JOHNNY'S
LEMONADE STAND

How You Can START-UP Your Own Business

For Daniel,

Enjoyed Having
you in my Class,

Bo Worthy

BO WORTHY

Go Jazz

Cover Photographer: Matthew Worthy
Cover Design: Katie Frederick
Cover Model: Stewart Thomas

ISBN: 1-4392-3735-2
ISBN-13: 9781439237359

www.createspace.com/1000247697

TABLE OF CONTENTS

DEDICATION

This book is dedicated to my children, Chas, Matthew, Victoria, and Allie.

My children are extraordinary (please notice I didn't say perfect). My sons have grown into outstanding young men and my daughters are beautiful and talented. Chas lives life with purpose and passion. Matthew seeks out adventure and has a positive impact on everyone he touches. Victoria was born to lead and has determination to die for. Allie's intensity lights up everyone around her.

I love each of you deeply.

ACKNOWLEDGEMENT

Writing a book is a challenge and a challenge that I could not have met without the help of countless individuals.

I could not have begun this writing journey without the opportunities you provided, the subtle lessons you taught me, and your wisdom that guided and matured me.

Thank you Booksurge for your unbridled professionalism, and your ability to perfectly direct every step of the publishing path.

Thank you, Thank you, Thank you Renae Venable for your countless hours of editing, suggestions, and encouragement. I needed your caliber of intelligence. I trusted you and the book is better for it.

Thank you Charles and Dannie Lou, my mom and dad, for believing in me and teaching me I could do anything at an early age.

Thank you Jesus.

INTRODUCTION

While serving as Mayor of Eclectic, a small town in central Alabama, from 1992-2000, I was occasionally asked to speak to different groups of people. I always enjoyed talking enthusiastically about our quaint town, my ideas to grow the town, and our bright future.

Simultaneous with being Mayor of Eclectic, I was also a founder and one of the owners of Hercules Bags (an actual paying job).

While sitting in my Hercules Bags' office one afternoon in the summer of 1999, I received a phone call from Miss Clara Booth. I had known and admired her for years as had everyone in Eclectic. Miss Clara (all women in the South get a "Miss" in front of their name regardless of marital status) worked with the local summer school program.

The kids in summer school were there for a reason; they hadn't paid attention in class the first time around and they had failed. The only way to keep up with their classmates was to take summer school classes.

One of Miss Clara's responsibilities was to get community leaders to give a speech to this wayward group and she asked me if I would be willing to talk to them. I told her I would do my civic duty by pointing them toward the straight and narrow and we set a date for me to come and speak.

Upon arriving at the school, Miss Clara met me in the hall and thanked me for coming. She immediately started apologizing for what she was sure was about to happen. She said the kids would probably not pay attention, that they would talk while I was speaking, and that some of them would just put their heads down and go to sleep. In short, they were all slackers who could care less about anything, especially a talk about city government.

I told Miss Clara I could handle it and asked her how long she wanted me to talk. She said she thought thirty minutes or so would be all they could stand.

As we walked into the classroom, something inside of me said change directions and talk about something other than being Mayor of Eclectic.

I listened to my inner voice.

I opened the talk with this line. "Hi, my name is Bo Worthy and I am Mayor of Eclectic. Miss Clara asked me to talk to you today about government and being a good citizen, but I am going to do something different."

And then, I asked a question that I have used numerous times since that day.

"How many of you would like to make a $100 this Saturday?"

All the kids in the class sat up in their chairs, sharpened their focus and raised their hands!

Finally, somebody was about to speak their language. MONEY!

For the next forty-five minutes, I gave a nonstop, high-spirited and totally impromptu business lesson on how to run a lemonade stand. You could have heard a pin drop. These kids had never heard anyone tell them they could own their own business and make their own money.

For the most part, the only thing they had ever been told was that they were losers headed for the scrapheap of failure.

On a black dusty chalkboard, I showed them how simple business really is; and I told them that if they wanted to run their own business, they could do it.

When I finished talking, I asked if there were any questions. Several students raised their hands and the business session went on for another ten to fifteen minutes.

Miss Clara finally had to interrupt and get the class back on track for their next hour of study. She thanked me in front of the class and then followed me out into the hall.

I will never forget what I saw next as I turned around to thank her for inviting me.

Tears were streaming down her face. She told me how she had never before seen them behave so well and be so attentive. I could tell she was overwhelmed with the joy of knowing her students had been touched. They got it and they believed it.

I told her how much I enjoyed having an impact and being so well received for such an off the cuff talk.

A couple of months later, I got asked to speak to another group about the same age. The only difference was they were private school kids who had a totally different background than the first group. They were smart, and most came from well-to-do families.

I used the same speech, the same chalkboard examples, and the same "you can do it" high spirited tone.

I was stunned. They reacted the exact same way. They loved being told they could make $100 and then shown how to do it.

The speech was simple: Teach them how, show them the path, give them a gentle kick in the seat of the pants, and get out of their way.

From that day forward, I knew I was onto something.

I learned that deep down, regardless of their background, most people just want to understand how to do something for themselves. As the great writer/speaker John Maxwell once said, "Everybody wants to be somebody."

As time passed and I returned to the full time world of entrepreneurship after serving 8 years as Mayor, I realized I wanted to get that message crafted into a book.

The message is simple. Anyone, regardless of age, income, education, or gender can own their own business.

"Johnny's Lemonade Stand" is a lively fictional story which takes Johnny Mac Williams through several stages of discovery that ultimately lead him to start his own business.

Like any real life entrepreneurial story, this one has comedy, sadness, anxiety, overconfidence, failure, and success. In the end, you will be inspired.

I have started and led several businesses from scratch over the past eighteen years. I know how to do a start-up. It's very simple to do, but it can be very hard taking the first step and getting started. If you've never done it, it just seems overwhelming and out of reach.

Relax, just like Johnny, once you get started, you will discover how much fun it is and how powerful and freeing it is to create your own wealth.

As you follow Johnny's journey, you will begin to discover for yourself what it takes and how to do it. By the end of the story, you will have all the basic tools.

While the story is about a fourteen year old boy, the business principles are timeless. It's a great read for any age and an especially good read for young people. It will set you on the right path for financial success in the world of business. It's absolutely perfect for anyone who is considering starting up a business. It will give you perspective.

Success and Survival in business are other matters entirely and both these characteristics require a different and more mature skill set. Just as I have done with Start-up, I will cover Success and Survival in two upcoming additions of the "Johnny's Lemonade Stand" series of books.

Enjoy.

CHAPTER 1
HOW LOW CAN YOU GO

"You find what you're looking for," Johnny's mother said sternly and loudly as Johnny moped around the house, looking under every stick of furniture for his baseball glove.

"I'll find it Mom," Johnny said somberly.

How could this happen? He had just used it on Thursday to play catch, and now it was gone. He was sure he had thrown it in the hall corner with the family collection of shoes, umbrellas, caps and other stuff, but it was nowhere to be found.

Johnny's mom, Lou, short for Louise, had watched this scene play out many, many times over the years. She knew the glove would show up eventually, so she just went about her routine and let Johnny resume his "find the missing glove" campaign.

No sooner had Johnny resumed the search in the bottomless hall corner, than he heard the soft thump of leather landing behind him on the wooden floor.

"You owe me," scowled Bets as she kicked the glove toward Johnny.

"Where did you find it?" Johnny asked smartly, knowing his sister had probably known where it had been all along.

"Where you left it," said Bets as she left the scene, quickly as she came.

Bets, fifteen, drove Johnny nuts. She had been named after their grandmother, and her real name was Betsy. She was the worst possible older sister any brother could have. She had the perfect trifecta going that just made Johnny crazy. She always found his "lost" glove, she always brought home better grades, and somehow she always had money. For a kid brother, it couldn't get any worse than that.

To make matters even worse, Johnny heard a car pull up in the driveway and knew her friends were there to take her to the movies for the second time this weekend while he sat at home for yet another weekend, broke and penniless again.

He hadn't meant for this to happen so quickly after his recent birthday bonanza. Just five weeks ago when he turned fourteen, Johnny had gotten $150 in birthday money. It was the most he had ever received for a birthday or Christmas, and he thought his ship had come in. He even called his best friends, Jimmy and Tony, and bragged he was now "rich."

The birthday cards filled with cash had come from the whole family tree—aunts, uncles, cousins, and most importantly, Grandma and Grandpa Williams. Johnny always counted on them for the big bills, and they didn't let him down. When Johnny opened the card from Grandpa and Grandma Williams, out fell two brand new "Jacksons."

Grandpa had always called money by the president pictured on the bills. Over the years, he had used birthday and Christmas gifts as a way to teach Johnny and Bets about American history. Grandpa was a retired high school principal who had taught history for twenty years before becoming principal at Truman High School. When the school was built in 1955, it was named after President Truman, who Grandpa thought should be on a bill of his own.

Grandpa always made Johnny answer history questions before he let him open the card. This year's question had been a little tricky. Johnny had to name a current baseball player and music composer who shared the same first name as the president on the twenty-dollar bill. The first step was to remember which president was on the twenty-dollar bill, which was easy, Andrew Jackson. The next part of answering the question was easy as well, since one of Johnny's favorite baseball players was Andruw Jones who had won several Golden Gloves playing center field, the same position Johnny played.

Part three was a disaster. Johnny had no clue what a music composer did much less the actual name of a modern one. After multiple clues from the whole family, which included Lloyd's of London insurance, the Webber charcoal grill, and some play about a phantom, Johnny was able to patch together Andrew Lloyd Webber even though he had no clue who this man was. Grandpa finally succumbed and just let Johnny open the card.

Johnny had told himself that day as the money piled up on the coffee table that he was going to save some of those "Jacksons." After Christmas Johnny had told himself the same thing, and that promise lasted a whopping two weeks until he was broker than broke. Ah, but this time was going to be different, Johnny had thought. He was going to follow through on his good intentions. Some things just never change. Four weeks after his birthday, Johnny was broke again. How could this happen?

Johnny began to think back about the past four weeks, which had included several trips to Frank's Batting Cage &

Outdoor Sports, the mall, and the movies. Then he knew where the money had gone.

"Johnny!" yelled his mom, "Jimmy is on the phone for you."

Johnny, brought back to reality in an instant, knew this was a call he didn't want to take. He had a feeling Jimmy was going to ask him if he wanted to go somewhere and hook up with Tony for an evening of fun.

The fun wasn't going to be the problem. Affording it was the problem. While Johnny's mind raced about what Jimmy wanted, he sheepishly said hello.

The next two minutes ranked in the top ten all-time losers for Johnny. Jimmy said Tony was meeting him at Castle Mountain for the grand opening in a couple of hours, and he was just making sure Johnny was going. Johnny sat there stunned, unable to speak. He had completely forgotten that April 1st was the grand opening, and they had planned on all going together.

Johnny stumbled around for what seemed like hours trying to think of some excuse to tell Jimmy. Finally, after being unable to muster the courage to tell the truth, he just told Jimmy he would call him back in an hour.

Johnny hung up the phone and slumped down into his dad's favorite chair, about as dejected as a fourteen-year-old boy could get. His two best friends were going to one of the biggest events in his lifetime, and he had not set aside any money. He had forgotten about the grand opening being today, and he knew it would cost a "Jackson" to get in.

The Rockhall Construction Company had been building the monster of an entertainment complex for over a year. It was the size of two football fields, and they advertised it to have everything. Nobody had been inside, but word on the street was that if you could imagine it, Castle Mountain had it—rock climbing, a hundred-foot free-fall slide, rollerblading, skateboarding, bumper cars, blast music, video games, live arcade, virtual sports, a batting cage with radar, and some kind of new game that they promised no kid had ever seen before.

Johnny needed $20 fast.

His parents were very generous, but Johnny knew better than to ask this time. Just last week, Lou and Billy had coughed up $100 for baseball registration. This had caused a big stink because Johnny had forgotten to tell his mom about the early registration period that would have cost only $80. She was furious over having to pay the extra $20 because of his forgetfulness. Luckily for Johnny, when Billy asked Lou why the fee seemed higher this year, she just said there were new "administrative fees" and left it at that. She had saved Johnny from the wrath of Dad, who had just mailed in the family taxes the day before and was none too happy about having to give Uncle Sam so many of his "Franklins."

Johnny's dad worked hard in downtown Belleville at the Williams' family hardware store with his brothers Ted and Nathan. Regularly, he reminded Johnny about the value of a dollar and how difficult it was to earn a living in these "tough" times.

When the topic of money came up around Dad, Johnny usually just tried to find a way out of the room rather than hear the lecture.

Johnny's costly forgetfulness had put him in no-man's-land with his parents. His needs were great, but the chance of getting everything he wanted was clearly not very good. Combined with the fact that he was going to need some new cleats for opening day of baseball practice on Monday, this could mean only one thing. A difficult choice had arrived: get the cleats, or go to Castle Mountain.

Coach Hill had told all the players they would need to get the new "Basebusters" down at Frank's Batting Cage & Sporting Goods Store. Basebusters were the latest, greatest shoe, and Coach Hill had arranged with Frank's for the team members to get a 20 percent discount if they bought shoes before Monday. There was no way Johnny could risk not telling his mom about the discount. This meant she was going to have to buy them today because Frank's was closed on Sundays.

Jimmy and Tony had already gotten their Basebusters, and Johnny didn't want to be the only player at practice without the new shoes. He had been waiting for the right moment to tell his mom he would need new shoes, and now the time had come. He couldn't wait any longer. It was now noon on Saturday. Frank's would be closing at three o'clock, and Castle Mountain was opening at two.

This nightmare was getting worse by the minute.

Suddenly, Bets yelled from the top of the stairs for Johnny to come up to her room. She said she needed him. Johnny's mind started working again as he headed up the stairs to see what his sister and her friends, Brooke and VJ, needed. Maybe Bets would let him borrow the $20 from one of her three special jars that she kept in the top drawer of her dresser.

She had labeled them SPEND, SAVE, and SHARE. Johnny knew for a fact that she had over $200 in the save jar. (He had peeked one time.)

When he got up to the room, all three girls were sitting on the fat, beaded throw cushions that Bets had gotten for Christmas. Bets told Johnny to close the door and sit down.

Johnny sat down and coolly said, "What's up?"

"We need a little favor."

"What kind of favor?", Johnny asked nervously.

"We need you to make a phone call," answered Bets, in an almost giggly voice. "And it will be worth $20 to you. We need to know which movie theatre the football players are going to tonight to watch *Remember the Titans*.

Johnny couldn't believe his ears. He was about to be paid to do a little investigative work for his sister and her boy crazy friends. It was as if she knew exactly how much he needed to make his day the perfect Saturday. Johnny said OK faster than he could swing at a fastball at Frank's Batting Cage.

There were two theatres showing the movie. Both were about a twenty-five-minute drive from Johnny's house. One was due south and the other northeast, making them fifty minutes apart. If the girls chose the wrong theatre, there would be no football players to "run into" and no time to get to the other theatre before the movie started.

Johnny knew exactly who to call. Their third baseman's name was Ernie, and his older brother Ben played linebacker for the varsity football team. He was the defensive captain, and he would surely be in on a team movie trip.

Johnny told Bets he would be right back and headed off to his room to call Ernie and get the scoop. Within two minutes, he was back in her room with the answer. "They are going to Belleville Commons to watch the six o'clock movie," Johnny proudly announced, as if he had just solved a crime. "Now give me my money."

What happened next made Johnny so mad he couldn't see straight for an hour.

"I never said I was going to pay you $20. I said it would be worth $20 to you," said Bets. "Do you remember that

$20 you borrowed from me the week before your birthday so you could go to Frank's Batting Cage with Jimmy? You told me you would pay me back with some of your birthday money. Well, consider your debt paid."

Johnny's face began to turn red. There was a reason his sister had $200 in her SAVE jar. She was smart and savvy, and she had gotten the best of him again. Yet, he knew she was right. He had totally forgotten to pay her back with his birthday money. To make matters worse, Johnny couldn't tell his mom about the injustice of what just happened because she had strictly forbidden Johnny from borrowing money because of his past "forgetfulness" in repaying his debts. His mom didn't know about the latest $20 Bets had lent him, and Johnny certainly wasn't going to tell her now.

Johnny turned, stormed out of the room, and slammed the door behind him even though he knew Bets had said "worth $20" from the beginning.

Somehow, the forgiveness of his debt didn't provide much satisfaction.

There was only one final path to pursue—throw caution to the wind and ask his mom for both the $20 and for the new Basebuster shoes. As Johnny headed down the stairs to put his new plan into action, he had a frightful thought.

What if his mom thought he was acting greedy and slammed the door on both requests? The thought of not getting anything had never really entered his mind, but after his ordeal with Betsy, his confidence was totally shot.

He stopped just short of the kitchen door as the reality of the situation finally settled in on him. It was Basebusters or Castle Mountain. He would never get both.

Johnny called Jimmy and gave him the news. He never explained to Jimmy why he couldn't go, and thankfully,

Jimmy didn't press too hard. Johnny suspected Jimmy knew the real reason and didn't want to make it any worse by taunting him about it.

After the call, he asked his mom if she would get him the shoes when she went shopping that afternoon. Grudgingly, she said she would if Johnny promised they would last all season and that he wouldn't lose them.

He never even brought up Castle Mountain.

Later that afternoon, he heard Bets, VJ, and Brooke come down the stairs talking about the movie and maybe going to Castle Mountain afterwards. He couldn't even look at them as they passed right by him in the family room and headed out the door.

Johnny just wanted one of the worst days of his life to be over. It seemed like nothing had gone right. He was broke and humiliated. All his friends were at the grand opening of Castle Mountain while he sat at home with Mom, Dad, and the family dog, Martina.

How low could he go?

Well, at least he had some Basebusters for Monday's practice.

CHAPTER 2
YOU REAP WHAT YOU SOW

The ride to church seemed especially long. Bets couldn't stop talking about all the people who were at the grand opening of Castle Mountain. Johnny just stared blankly out the window while Bets told his parents about every fun game and adventure in the place.

"I thought you were going to go to the opening with Jimmy and Tony," said Johnny's mom. She obviously didn't know about Johnny's dire financial circumstances, and Johnny was really struggling to explain why he hadn't gone.

His saving grace was the short ride to the church. They were now pulling into the parking lot. He was off the hook.

Johnny's day took a turn for the better as soon as he opened his car door. There stood Mr. C., one of his favorite people in the entire world and definitely the best Sunday School teacher at Saint Peter's.

Mr. C., who must have been in his seventies but looked fifty, taught thirteen- to fifteen-year-old boys at Saint Peter's. All the guys loved him. He was smart and funny, and his lessons were never boring. He always had maps and pictures from places he taught about and sometimes he brought funny tasting food from the places they studied.

As a marine, Mr. C. had traveled the world, and he was very good at making Bible stories come to life. He could get the twelve to fifteen students in his class to see the "big picture" as he would say it.

"Good to see ya, Johnny," said Mr. C. in his usual cheery voice. "I had a good week, and I can't wait to share it with you guys in class this morning."

Johnny couldn't wait either as he followed Mr. C. up the steps to the room where their group met each week.

After about ten minutes, all the guys had arrived, and Mr. C. said it was time to start. Even though this was a lively group of boys, all the chatter died down immediately when Mr. C. spoke. Everyone in the class fully respected him, and there were hardly ever any behavioral problems. Once, Jimmy had gotten a little unruly, and Mr. C. took him out into the hall. When they came back in, Jimmy's face was white as ashes.

To this day, Johnny didn't know what Mr. C. said in that hall. He just knew Jimmy never acted ugly in Sunday School again, and neither did anyone else.

Mr. C. began the lesson by asking if anyone's family in the class was going to have a garden this summer. Seven kids raised their hands, and Mr. C. asked what their favorite vegetable was going to be. For the most part, corn was on everybody's list.

Mr. C. then asked who was actually going to help their parents prepare and plant the garden. Only two kids raised their hands. Mr. C. gave them heaping praise for being hard workers and willing to help their parents.

He then turned his attention to the reason he had asked the question. He said the title of today's lesson was "You Reap What You Sow."

Over the next thirty minutes, Mr. C. taught the class the importance of understanding what reaping and sowing meant. He was very good at taking a biblical truth and helping young boys understand what it meant, and today was no exception.

This lesson about reaping and sowing was completely holding Johnny's attention. Johnny would never tell Mr. C., but sometimes he had daydreamed in his class.

Not today.

Mr. C. read from the scripture and told the group the biblical meaning of reaping what you sow.

He then told the class he wanted to share some practical examples of what reaping and sowing meant to a teenager that they might recognize in their own lives.

Mr. C. started with the positives.

He used the example that more practice would lead to a better performance during the baseball game, and Johnny immediately understood this example. He loved baseball, and he had spent lots of time at Frank's Batting Cage so that he would be a better hitter come game time.

When Mr. C. said that studying your homework would lead to better grades, Johnny got the point. When he said that helping someone in need could lead to a lifelong friendship, Johnny completely understood the connection.

Then Mr. C. discussed how poor choices also have consequences.

He talked about unwise behavior, wasteful spending, being lazy, and all the bad things that usually followed each one of these choices.

At the end of the lesson, Mr. C. asked the class to consider what circumstances in their lives were turning out well because of good choices and what was not going well because of bad choices.

Johnny's mind was racing.

Where was his life headed? Was he doing anything well? What was he doing poorly?

Suddenly, all kinds of lights were going off in Johnny's head.

He began to think about how humiliated he felt yesterday when Jimmy called and he couldn't be honest with him about being broke. He had spent all his money as fast as he could and hadn't saved any at all.

Johnny was reaping what he had sown, and for the first time he owned up to the fact that he was the root cause of his own misery.

Johnny could hardly wait for the end of church to get a chance to talk to Mr. C. one-on-one. It seemed like Pastor Miller's sermon would last forever even though it probably was just the usual forty-five minutes.

As soon as Miss Fulton hit the last note on the organ, Johnny sprinted for the back door to see Mr. C. He could barely contain himself. He just had to know. He just had to know the answer to the question that had been running through his mind for the past hour.

Johnny couldn't get the question off his mind as he worked his way through the crowd to find Mr. C. Suddenly, as he maneuvered behind Pastor Miller shaking hands with the Roberts clan, he spotted Mr. C.

He was busy talking to Miss Simpson, and Johnny knew better than to interrupt Miss Simpson. Miss Simpson was the church lady who did good deeds for everyone and was just involved in everything. Just two weeks ago, she had caught Johnny and Tony playing hide-and-seek in the church sanctuary. When it was Johnny's turn to hide, he had chosen the baptismal pool, which had always been a popular spot to hide.

Little did he know, Miss Simpson was cleaning out the baptismal pool that afternoon.

When the door swung open, Johnny was sure Tony had found him, and he yelled, "Surprise!"

Miss Simpson screamed, dropped the cleaning bucket of bleach, and fell backwards all in one fell swoop. Stuff went everywhere.

Johnny ran for his life.

One hour later, Miss Simpson called Johnny's mom, and he was sure he was dead. When Lou, Johnny's mom, hung up the phone, she began to laugh hysterically.

Lou found the thought of Miss Simpson with a bleach bucket on her head just too funny to get serious about punishing Johnny. However, it did end the hide-and-seek games in the church sanctuary.

Finally, Miss Simpson finished talking to Mr. C., and Johnny followed him out to his car. He had never been nervous about talking to Mr. C. before, but for some reason, this time was different.

Mr. C. noticed Johnny following him and asked him if he enjoyed the Sunday School lesson. Johnny said yes and told Mr. C. that he would like to talk to him some more about the lesson. He also said he had a question for Mr. C.

Mr. C. asked Johnny what he was doing that afternoon and if he would like to come over to his house after lunch. He told Johnny he had something special he wanted to show him and that they could also talk about whatever was on Johnny's mind.

Johnny happily agreed to be at Mr. C.'s house at two o'clock.

He didn't know what Mr. C. wanted to show him, but he sure knew what he wanted to ask Mr. C.

CHAPTER 3
WISDOM FROM A MASTER

Sunday lunch was always a big deal at the Williams' house, and today was no exception. The men had chosen their customary chairs at the table—Johnny's dad, Billy, on one end of the table and Grandpa Williams on the other. They had already gotten into the weekly argument over politics and who was going to win the baseball pennants before they said the blessing and passed the potatoes.

This was Johnny's favorite meal each week. Grandma Williams always brought dessert, and Lou, who was a great cook, would always cook a huge meal so Billy could take the leftovers to work all week for lunch.

Lou had made meatloaf today, which was one of Johnny's favorites. Grandma Williams had brought fresh apple pie, and Grandpa had given up one of his "Hamiltons" to buy the Willie's premium golden vanilla ice cream to go on top.

Johnny loved Willie's golden vanilla!

Johnny could hardly sit still thinking about going over to Mr. C.'s at two o'clock. He kept looking up at the clock on the wall to see what time it was.

"Do you have somewhere to go? You seem antsy," Bets questioned Johnny.

"None of your business," Johnny shot back before realizing that probably wasn't the wisest choice of words to use at the dinner table in front of the whole family.

Right on cue, Lou chimed in immediately, "Johnny Mac Williams, you watch your mouth. And by the way, where are you going?"

"Sorry Mom, but she is always messing with me," Johnny said. "Mr. C. invited me over to his house this afternoon to show me something special. I think he is going to have another unveiling."

Upon hearing that, Grandpa asked Grandma to "unveil" the apple pie, and lunch resumed as normal.

Lunch was always over at one thirty whether everyone had finished eating or not because that was when Billy and Grandpa's favorite TV show came on each week.

Johnny needed to spend twenty-five minutes doing something, or he was going to go crazy waiting to go to Mr. C.'s house. It was only a five-minute bike ride over to Mr. C.'s, so Johnny offered to help clear the table to pass the time. Needless to say, Lou almost passed out. She could not remember the last time Johnny had helped with the dishes.

As Johnny and his mom cleaned the dishes, the usual hoots and hollers were coming out of the family room.

Johnny's dad and grandpa loved boxing, and they always watched Boxing Greats, a TV show, at one thirty on Sunday afternoons. Grandpa had worked his way through college by cleaning Shorty's Gym every night and had developed quite the love of boxing as a result.

"Get up, Gus! Get up!" Johnny heard his dad yell from the family room, knowing that meant Jerry had knocked down Gus.

"He's gettin' up, Billy! He's gettin' up! Gus ain't no quitter!" Grandpa hollered back as they both were now yelling at Gus to get up and crush Jerry the Barbarian.

Finally, at ten minutes until two o'clock, Johnny couldn't stand the wait any longer. He jumped on his bike and took off to Mr. C.'s.

As Johnny rode up into Mr. C.'s yard, he dropped his bike beside the huge oak tree that was right up against the front porch.

"Hello, Johnny," said Darlene, Mr. C.'s wife, who was watering the flowers that were all over the front porch.

"Your flowers sure are pretty, Miss Darlene," Johnny said as he walked up onto the porch. "My mom kills flowers," Johnny continued as he opened the front door and went inside.

"Clarence is out back in the shop, Johnny, and don't touch the cookies in the kitchen. They're cooling," Darlene said as Johnny disappeared into the house.

Mr. C. hated for anyone to call him Clarence. The only two people who ever did that were Darlene and Pastor Miller.

Mr. C. and Darlene had a beautiful yard and a grand home that was the envy of everyone in Belleville. Old, massive oak trees lined the perimeter of the yard, skirted by a white picket fence that Mr. C. had built himself.

The view from the back porch was like a Norman Rockwell painting. The lawn was dark green, and Darlene, who loved roses, had placed twelve small rose beds around the yard. They were in full bloom. Johnny had asked her one time why she had so many rose beds, and she had told him she liked them "by the dozen."

There were two buildings in the backyard—the shop and the boathouse. Johnny had been in them both many times before. The boathouse was just a short walk down a rock path that led to the shores of Lake Evers.

Everybody in Belleville loved to spend time at Lake Evers during the summer when school was out and the water was warm enough to go swimming.

The boathouse was where Mr. C. kept his vintage 1950-model speedboat. It was a classic, and he referred to it as his baby. It was twenty-four feet long, 100 percent wood, and painted solid blue. Mr. C. had named it The Blue Rose.

Several times a year, Mr. C. would have all the boys from his class come over for a ride on Lake Evers in the The Blue Rose. All Johnny's friends loved the boat rides, but their favorite thing to do was to swing out over the lake on the rope Mr. C. had hung from one of the oak limbs stretching out over the water.

Once, Jimmy got scared and didn't let go of the rope after he had pushed off from shore. Needless to say, when Jimmy came swinging back in, it was like a bowling ball knocking over pins as kids were scattered everywhere. Jimmy didn't get another rope turn the rest of the summer as all the kids teased him about not being able to let go.

The shop was a few feet from the boathouse. It was a large A-frame wooden building with a small front door and a ten-foot-wide rollup door on the backside.

As Johnny opened the door, Mr. C. said, "Hello, Johnny. You're right on time." Johnny knew the routine. He had been in Mr. C.'s shop many times before. Don't be late. Don't touch the boats. Don't mess with the tools, and don't interrupt Mr. C.'s stories.

Mr. C.'s shop looked like a boat museum. He had everything: submarines, aircraft carriers, PT boats, battleships, cruisers, fishing boats, and many more. You name it, and he had it. And he had at least one from every country that had floated a navy in the past three hundred years. He was an avid collector and builder and had built over half of his models himself. Every hand-built model was an exact replica of the original design.

He was an amazing craftsman. Local newspapers and regional magazines always featured his models after an unveiling.

Johnny knew something new was about to be unveiled when Mr. C. motioned him to the far wall and told him to go to the blue tarp and grab one of the ends. Whatever they were about to see was sitting on three large tables that Mr. C. used each week for his woodworking classes.

He usually had twenty-five to thirty people come every Tuesday night, and he taught them how to build birdhouses, refinish furniture, construct models from scratch, and build all kinds of stuff made out of wood.

Mr. C. went to the other end of the tarp, which must have been ten feet away and said, "On my count: one—two—three!"

Up came the tarp, and Johnny just stood there, unable to speak.

It was beautiful, and it was big.

Emblazoned across the hull was the single word that told the whole story: Titanic.

This thing was huge.

Johnny stood there mesmerized while Mr. C. began to tell the story.

"It's an exact replica that's eight feet long. I used the same materials that were used on the original ship. Miss Simpson actually helped me with the furniture and the people figurines. She's coming over around three o'clock to take some pictures for the newspaper."

Mr. C. beamed with pride and began to show Johnny all the rooms of the ship. The hull opened up like a drawbridge so you could see inside the ship. Every room was exquisite in its detail. The ballroom. The dining room. The galley. The stairwells. The bedrooms. They were all fully outfitted with miniature furniture and people dressed in the time period of the early 1900s.

Johnny's favorite section was the outer deck with its beautiful wood floors and the small lifeboats dangling nearby.

In Johnny's humble opinion, this was by far the grandest vessel Mr. C. had ever built.

"How long did it take?" Johnny asked.

"Which part?" Mr. C. said, still beaming with pride. "Do you mean the building or the planning?"

"Well, I guess the building part," Johnny said.

"The building was really the easiest part," Mr. C. told Johnny. "That took about twelve months. It was the planning and acquiring all the materials that took the longest time—about three or four years I believe. Really, I started thinking about building it several years before that, so I probably have eight to ten years in this ship."

Johnny had heard Mr. C. talk about "dedication" many times over the past three years in their Sunday School class, and now he knew what dedication really meant.

Johnny suddenly realized how blessed he was to have been invited to the unveiling. Of all the people Mr. C. could have shown the ship to first, for some reason, Johnny had been the one.

He felt very special.

Johnny knew this was big. This was achievement. He couldn't even imagine how much work and effort had gone into the ship, and what could make somebody work that hard for so long.

"Why did you start something that you knew would take you so long to finish?" Johnny asked softly.

"Why do you play baseball?" Mr. C. asked Johnny as if to change the subject.

That's easy, Johnny thought. "Because I love it."

"Yes, and you are also good at it," Mr. C. said quickly. "Just because you love something doesn't mean you will be good at it. But when you love to do something and you are good at it, it can become your passion. Building ships is my passion."

Johnny and Mr. C. continued to walk around the Titanic and stop every couple of feet to admire a different section of the ship. At each stop, Johnny would ask a question, and Mr. C. would happily tell the story of why that section of the ship was important.

As they walked by each section, Johnny wondered to himself if he would ever develop a "passion" that would lead to something so grand.

Miss Simpson arrived right on time, as usual, and the picture taking began. She had Mr. C. pose in each picture alongside the ship. After ten or so pictures from every angle, Mr. C. had gotten his fill of smiling for the camera and invited us both inside for some lemonade and homemade cookies.

While Miss Simpson went into the kitchen to visit with Darlene, Johnny and Mr. C. sat down in the family room on a couple of stools that sat around the coffee table.

"So," said Mr. C., "tell me what's on your mind Johnny. You said after church that you wanted to discuss something."

With all the excitement of the ship unveiling, Johnny had completely forgotten about telling Mr. C. that he wanted to discuss something.

Johnny's mind started working again, and he remembered what it was he wanted to ask Mr. C.

If he could just spit it out.

CHAPTER 4
DISCOVERY

Now that Mr. C. had opened the door to talk about what was on Johnny's mind, Johnny knew he had to be totally honest. Mr. C. had a way of sniffing out the "whole truth and nothing but the truth," and Johnny was not about to play loose with the facts.

"Well, Mr. C.," Johnny started, "I haven't been doing so good with hanging onto my money, and your lesson this morning made me realize that it's my own fault."

"I'm glad you were paying attention this morning Johnny," said Mr. C., pleased that his lessons were finding a listening ear. "So what are you going to do about this problem?" he asked Johnny.

Johnny had never thought of himself as having a "problem."

"Well, I was kinda hoping you could give me some direction," said Johnny, now beginning to feel embarrassed about his condition and sharing it with somebody for the first time.

"Do you mind if I ask you a personal question Mr. C.?" Johnny asked shyly.

"No, not at all. You can ask me anything you want, Johnny," Mr. C. replied.

After a short stint of silence and heavy lemonade drinking, Johnny finally blurted out the question that had been on his mind all day.

"Are you rich?"

As soon as the words come out of Johnny's mouth, he wished he hadn't said them. For some reason, the spoken question just seemed awkward. It didn't come out the way he had thought it would, and now he felt foolish for asking it. The question caught Mr. C. by surprise even though he had told Johnny he could ask him anything.

For a brief moment Johnny was not even sure why he had asked the question, or better yet, why that particular question had settled on his mind after hearing about reaping what you sow in Sunday School.

Mr. C. continued to drink his lemonade and nibble on Darlene's homemade cookies. It was as if Johnny had thrown a fastball right at his head. He didn't know whether to duck or charge the mound.

After a minute or two, Mr. C. decided what to do.

Without answering the question, Mr. C. told Johnny to enjoy the goodies and that he would be right back. In a couple of minutes, he returned with a large photo album and opened it on the coffee table beside the lemonade and cookies.

At first Johnny was puzzled about where this moment was going. Mr. C. began showing Johnny pictures from his world travels when he was a marine for thirty years and the director of World Helpers for ten years.

For the next twenty minutes, Mr. C. showed Johnny picture after picture of dozens of places around the world that had one theme in common: they were all poor and underdeveloped countries where millions of people lived in poverty.

After retiring as a colonel in the Marine Corps, Mr. C. had spent ten years as the director for an organization called World Helpers. He had helped build orphanages, schools, and churches in the poorest countries in the world, and he wanted Johnny to see what real poverty looked like before answering his question. There was picture after picture of Mr. C. holding little children in front of the buildings he had helped build. Nothing more needed to be said as they turned page after page of the picture album.

When they had finished looking at the last picture, Mr. C. closed the album and said something that Johnny would never forget.

"From one American to another American, we're all rich."

Even though Johnny was only fourteen, he obviously understood what Mr. C. was saying and wished he could take back his question. It seemed so crude to him now.

"I guess what I meant to say was that, uh well, you know, you and Miss Darlene seem to have a lot of money, and ya'll have this big house on the lake, and you have all those model boats, and you travel all over the world," Johnny said, digging a deeper hole for himself.

Johnny suddenly had an awful thought. What if his mom and dad found out he was quizzing Mr. C. on how much money he had? He felt sick knowing his parents might ground him for a year for being so disrespectful.

Mr. C. knew what Johnny was trying to get at even though Johnny had stumbled so horribly in saying it.

"Johnny," said Mr. C., "Darlene and I have been very blessed throughout our lives, but there is a difference between being rich and having money."

Johnny was relieved Mr. C. had not gotten angry over his immature and probing question. Feeling like he was beginning to catch on to Mr. C.'s line of thought, he asked "How so?"

"Being rich is understanding the total value of what you have and who you are. For example, we have three children and seven grandchildren, and there is no amount of money that would be more important to me than they are. That makes us rich. We have been fortunate to be healthy all our lives. That makes us rich. Most importantly, we understand that God loves us just the way we are, and that makes us truly rich."

"Money is a part of being rich, but it is only a small part for Darlene and me," continued Mr. C. "We have so many other reasons to live that are higher priorities for us than making a lot of money. Don't get me wrong, Johnny—money is important, and it can open many opportunities for you. Just don't let the quest for it ruin your life."

Johnny was beginning to get it. Money was important, but that was not the only thing that made you rich.

"I understand the difference now," Johnny said. "I guess when I heard you talk about reaping what you sow, I just thought about the money part."

"Why do you think that is Johnny?" Mr. C. asked.

Johnny knew the answer to that question, but he was not real comfortable talking about his money woes. He also knew Mr. C. deserved an honest answer, as Mr. C. had been honest with him when he had posed a tough question.

Johnny jumped right into his own personal mess. "My problem is I don't have any money at all, and when I do get some for a birthday or Christmas, I just don't seem to be able to keep it. It seems like I have to ask Mom and Dad every week for something. I just wish I could do some things on my own without having to always ask them. This morning, when I heard you talking about reaping what you sow, you could have used me as your bad example. I sure have reaped what I have sowed, and I definitely got what was coming to me," Johnny said as Mr. C. listened intently.

"I am just tired of never having any money, and I am not sure what I need to be doing. The next time my friends call and want to do something fun, I don't won't to have to crawl under the couch and hide because I'm broke. I guess what I'm trying to say, Mr. C., is, well, I want to be like you. You have it all. I don't have anything," Johnny said.

After pouring his guts out, Johnny gulped down a huge swallow of lemonade and noticeably relaxed on the stool. He felt like he was a new man and had gotten a huge weight off his chest. He had never done that before.

He had never told his dad anything like that before, and he certainly had not told Jimmy and Tony about any of his problems. Johnny was not into drama. He didn't know where this new attitude about being honest with himself was coming from, but he was glad it was surfacing.

For some unknown reason, he just seemed comfortable telling Mr. C. about his problems.

Mr. C. was obviously flattered that Johnny thought so highly of him. He also knew this was a great opportunity to begin steering Johnny onto the road to self-reliance.

"Johnny, you just turned the corner," Mr. C. said as proudly as if he had unveiled another boat.

"What do you mean?" Johnny questioned.

"Well, think about it, Johnny. As I see it, you have discovered two things about yourself. First, you know you want to be able to do some things with your friends with your own money, and two, I heard you say you are willing to do something about it," Mr. C. replied.

"What do you think I should do next, Mr. C.?" Johnny asked excitedly.

"Have you thought about getting a job? Or better yet, Johnny, maybe you should start a business."

Johnny had thought about getting a job delivering newspapers with his bike one time. One of his friends at school had told him he could make $25 a week. When he discovered that he would have to get up every morning at four o'clock, seven days a week, he quickly decided that was not for him.

Starting a business? Wow! That was a totally radical thought.

Johnny had never thought of that before, and he felt intrigued by the whole idea.

"Do you really think I could run a business, Mr. C.? Starting a business seems like something an adult would do or a college person. It just seems complicated," Johnny said. "I mean, I am just fourteen. I'm not sure I even understand how a business works."

"Actually, Johnny, starting a business is very simple," Mr. C. responded eagerly. "Let's get some more lemonade, and I will tell you how it works."

CHAPTER 5
THE THREE-LEGGED STOOL

Johnny returned from the kitchen with a full plate of homemade cookies and a tall glass of cold lemonade. Miss Darlene had piled the cookies three high on his plate, and Johnny had just smiled, offering no resistance.

Mr. C. settled onto his stool then placed an empty stool between himself and Johnny. Johnny just assumed he was going to put his lemonade or cookies on the seat, but Mr. C. just sipped on his lemonade and looked at the empty stool.

"What do you see, Johnny?" asked Mr. C. as he gazed at the stool.

Johnny wasn't quite sure what Mr. C. meant, so he just said the obvious. "I see a stool."

"Tell me about the stool, Johnny," Mr. C. directed without looking up.

Johnny was still confused, but he knew Mr. C. was trying to make a point, so he played along.

"Well, it's brown, about three feet tall, and it has a round seat," Johnny said.

"Give me more details, Johnny," said Mr. C., beginning to smile.

"OK," Johnny said as he contemplated what apparently made this stool so special he had to analyze it. "It has three thick legs that make it strong enough to hold up my Uncle Joe."

"How big is your uncle Joe?" Mr. C. said, laughing.

"His nickname is Tex, short for Texas. He's big," Johnny said as they were both laughing now.

"You're starting to see it, Johnny," Mr. C. said as his serious voice returned. "What would happen if your uncle Joe was sitting on the stool and I kicked one of the three legs out from under it?"

"It would crash, and Uncle Joe definitely would need some help getting up off the floor," Johnny said as he imagined what a train wreck that would look like.

"But why would the stool fall over?" Mr. C. asked as if trying to prove something so simple a child could understand.

"Because it won't stand up on two legs," Johnny said.

"Exactly, and it won't stand up on one leg either, Johnny," Mr. C. said as he paused before making his next statement. "What makes the stool strong and able to stand is that it has three legs."

"What does a strong three-legged stool have to do with starting a business?" Johnny asked.

Mr. C. had Johnny right where he wanted him.

"Johnny, a good business is like a three-legged stool," said Mr. C. "It must have three strong legs to stand up and be strong."

"The first leg is the product leg," Mr. C. continued emphatically. "You must have something that has value."

"Mr. C.," Johnny interrupted, "what product do you have for your woodworking class?"

"That's an easy one Johnny," Mr. C. answered. "My product is my knowledge of how to build things, and I teach that to those who come to my class. When people pay me $20 for a two-hour session, they are buying my ability to teach them my knowledge of woodworking."

Johnny had never thought of the teaching of knowledge as a product, but now it made perfect sense.

"You see, Johnny, every business has to have a product that somebody will want whether the product is tangible or intangible," Mr. C. explained.

Johnny didn't want to sound dumb, but the tangible and intangible comment had confused him. He wasn't sure he understood what that meant, and so he just nodded his head as if to agree.

Fortunately, Mr. C. noticed Johnny's' confusion by the expression on his face and explained it in a way that anybody could understand.

Mr. C. continued, "Think of tangible products as things you can touch and feel—like food or clothes or cars or computers or boats. Think of intangible products as something you can't hold and feel, but you can see the benefit. For example, Darlene and I have to buy car insurance in case of an accident. You can't hold car insurance in your hand, but if we had a fender bender, it sure would be valuable. Like insurance, my ability to teach woodworking is an intangible product. My students don't leave the shop each Tuesday night with something in their hands; they leave with something in their minds they can use to build their own projects."

Johnny was really beginning to get into the three-legged stool. All kinds of light bulbs were going off in his head. As he glanced around the family room, he realized that everything was a product—the TV, the wall clock, the sofa, the magazine rack, the bookcase, the ceiling fan, the lamp, the rug. He was beginning to see everything with a completely new perspective.

"What's the second leg of the business stool?" Johnny asked, his eyes now totally focused again on Mr. C.

"The second leg is capital," Mr. C. said matter-of-factly.

Johnny wasn't sure what kind of capital Mr. C. was referring to, but he was quite sure he didn't mean Washington, DC. Mr. C. had a way of making you think, and Johnny knew by the way he was looking at him that Mr. C. was testing him.

"Well," started Johnny, "I am not sure, but are you talking about maybe a place where a business should be located?" Johnny came up with this answer because his mom, Lou, had once sold real estate, and she was always talking about "location, location, location."

Mr. C. appreciated Johnny's effort to explain the second leg of the business stool, but he offered a gentle correction.

"Well, Johnny, the location of a business can certainly be important, but that's not what I mean by capital," said Mr. C. as he confirmed Johnny's own hunch that he had given the wrong answer.

Johnny nodded politely as Mr. C. began to explain.

"Capital is everything you need to get your product to market. Take a farmer, for instance. He needs a tractor to plant his crops, day laborers to pick the harvest, and a big truck and trailer to haul it to market."

"Doesn't that take money to buy those tractors and trailers and pay those people?" Johnny asked, wondering where all the money came from to make businesses run.

"Johnny," said Mr. C. proudly, "you are really starting to understand how a business works. Yes, it takes a lot of money to start and run a big business or farm. However, most businesses start out small, and they use capital they already have on hand to get going. For example, if you were going to start a painting business and your dad had a ladder and some paintbrushes, he might let you borrow them to get started."

"Yeah, but I would still need to buy some paint, and that would take money," Johnny said.

"Yes, you're right," Mr. C. agreed. "It would take some money to get started, but not as much if you could use the existing capital you already have. Almost everyone already owns something that they could use as capital to start a business. For example, when I started my woodworking classes eight years ago, I just made room in my shop for some extra tables where students could work. I had been building my model boats for several years in that shop, and I had acquired a really good collection of tools over the years that I could use for the classes as well. I bought three sturdy tables for $120, I bought an ad in the Belleville Times for $50 to advertise the classes, and in one week, I was in business. Think about it, Johnny—a building and some tools that I already owned and $170 for tables and advertising. That was all the capital I needed to get started."

Johnny was grinning from ear to ear. He felt like he was in some kind of school with his own special teacher. This business lesson was better than any class in school he had ever taken. He was captivated by the way Mr. C. explained starting a business. It was so simple.

"Wait a minute," said Johnny, "you said there were three legs to the stool."

"That's right, I did. Now what do you think is the third leg? Remember, you now have a product and some capital—what's the last thing you need?" asked Mr. C.

Johnny was feeling pretty good about getting this leg right. Everything was pointing in one direction.

"Somebody has got to buy what you have," said Johnny loudly, totally sure his answer was at least close to the truth.

"Yes!" shouted Mr. C. "You got it! You have to have customers. That's the third leg."

Johnny was very relieved he had gotten it right. He felt good when Mr. C. gave him a high five.

"Johnny," Mr. C. said, "this is the most important and difficult leg of the business stool."

"What makes having customers so difficult?" Johnny wondered aloud, not knowing how naïve his question was.

"I'll tell you a secret, but you have to promise to never tell Darlene I told you, or she would skin me alive," Mr. C. whispered. There was not a man in Belleville who could skin Mr. C. alive, but Darlene always kept him in check.

Johnny's eyes lit up as he leaned forward to hear the secret. "Tell me, Mr. C., I promise I won't tell anyone."

"Customers are like wives—you can't live with them, and you can't live without them," Mr. C. said as both he and Johnny chuckled aloud.

Johnny didn't tell Mr. C. he had already heard his dad and grandpa use that line about wives at the Sunday dinner table many times before.

Continuing with his explanation of customers, Mr. C. said, "If you're selling red apples, they want green apples. If you have trucks, they want cars. If you can build a house in ninety days, they want it in thirty days. Customers are just very difficult to please. You just have to work very hard at understanding what they want and keep trying every day to make them happy."

Mr. C. continued explaining the customer leg. "When I started my woodworking class, I thought I would teach everyone how to build fancy model boats. You know what

I found out? Most of my students just wanted to learn how to build a birdhouse or a flowerpot, so I had to change my direction to keep the customers happy and coming back. After a few sessions, I learned to listen to what the customers were saying they wanted to learn to build, and now my shop is full of happy customers every Tuesday.

"With any business, you have to be willing to listen to the customers, and you have to be willing to give the customers what they want. People who own businesses stumble over this leg of the stool a lot more than the other two legs. You just cannot be stubborn with customers. You have to be willing to change as the times change, or you won't have any customers," Mr. C. concluded.

Mr. C. was now talking much slower as he gave Johnny one final thought on starting a business. "Just remember, Johnny, you have to have all three legs for the business to work. If any of the legs gets knocked out, the stool will fall, and the business will fail."

Mr. C. slid back on his stool and relaxed, which indicated to Johnny that the business lesson of the three-legged stool was now over.

Johnny couldn't get over how simple it was to start a business.

Product. Capital. Customers. A three-legged stool. Could it really be that simple?

Tons of thoughts and questions were running through Johnny's mind. He had done some exciting things in his short fourteen years of living, but never anything as adventurous as launching a business.

Johnny had one question that he had to ask. "If starting a business is so simple, why do most people work for somebody else?"

"That's a very good question Johnny," said Mr. C. "There are probably a lot of reasons. Sometimes people aren't ready. Sometimes people feel like they don't know enough or don't have enough capital. But I think mostly it's just that people are too afraid to try. They think it might fail, and they don't want to risk their capital. Personally, I think everyone should own a business at least once in his or her life. It's a challenge, and I have enjoyed it every bit as much as anything I've ever done."

The next statement came out of Johnny's mouth before he could even think about what he was saying.

"I want to start my own business, Mr. C.," Johnny said, as serious as he had ever been. "I think I'm ready to try."

"Well, OK Johnny, what kind of business do you think you will start?" Mr. C. asked supportively.

"I don't know," replied Johnny. "What do you think I could do?"

"Let's go in the kitchen and get a refill, and then we can talk about it some more," Mr. C. suggested as they both climbed off their stools and headed toward the kitchen door.

Darlene and Miss Simpson were still in the kitchen, sitting at the counter where Darlene kept her magazines and the daily newspaper. It was also where the phone was located, and that made the counter the spot to be.

Darlene also loved the view from the counter. Mr. C. had built a large bay window that overlooked the whole backyard and most of Lake Evers. Every time Johnny came over, he knew he would probably find Miss Darlene at the counter reading something or talking on the phone.

"I suppose you two want some more lemonade," Darlene said as they slid their empty glasses over the counter.

"Yep, I think one more will do it for me," said Mr. C. as he and Johnny stood there with goofy grins on their faces.

"Your lemonade is the best I have ever had, Miss Darlene," Johnny said.

Darlene began to pour the lemonade and laughingly said, "Let me see now—that is two glasses for Clarence and three for you, Johnny. If my lemonade is so good, I should be charging ya'll a dollar a glass. I'd be well on my way to getting rich as much as ya'll drink."

Bells. Bright lights. Angelic choirs singing. You name it—it was all happening at once.

Johnny and Mr. C. immediately turned and looked at one another. It was as if they thought the same thing at the same time.

The fog in Johnny's mind about what kind of business he should start cleared up in an instant.

Johnny could see a table with an umbrella, a sign, rows of glasses filled with ice-cold lemonade, and more customers than he could count lined up for a city block.

He had found what he was looking for. It was too good to be true. Mr. C. had just said that business was simple, but Johnny never expected to have figured it out so quickly.

"Miss Darlene, can you teach me how to make lemonade as good as yours?" Johnny asked.

"Sure, Johnny," said Darlene, a little puzzled, "but what are you going to do with my lemonade recipe? You know, it has been a family secret for generations. It's very special."

If Miss Darlene only knew what was up Johnny's sleeve.

Johnny Mac Williams was about to be a businessman.

CHAPTER 6
SKIN IN THE GAME

On the bike ride back home, a million thoughts went through Johnny's mind about what he should be doing next. After his revelation in Miss Darlene's kitchen, Mr. C. gave him some more pointers about getting started and sent Johnny on his way.

Now, it was all up to Johnny. Was he really going to start a business? Or was this lemonade stand idea just going to fade into the sunset as had some of Johnny's other plans over the years like saving a little money and improving his grades?

Nope, Johnny meant it. He was as focused as he had ever been on anything, and for some strange reason, he just knew he was going to see this idea all the way through.

Johnny knew he would need some help in putting his lemonade stand together. The first thing he had to decide was who he could really trust to help him get it started. Somebody who would believe in him no matter what happened and who wouldn't tell him "I told you so" if all three legs collapsed under his stool.

Johnny's dad, Billy, was a really good father and had helped Johnny with many fun projects over the years. They had built several tree houses and soapbox derby cars together. Billy had also taught Johnny how to play baseball and had been the local scout leader for several years. Johnny knew his dad really loved him and that he would be willing to help, but there was just one major problem. This was spring, and it was the busiest time of year for the hardware store. The store would be open six days a week until seven o'clock each night until the end of June and Billy had to be there every day. He just would not have any time for the next three months.

Johnny's thoughts switched to his sister, Bets. Bets had capital and lots of it. She might let him borrow some money to get his lemonade stand up and running. Then, an unusual thought came across Johnny's mind. If he could figure out a way to get started without asking his sister, that might change the way she viewed her little brother. As much as he needed her capital, he wanted her respect even more. This was his chance to earn it. Bets was out.

That left Johnny's mom, Lou. Johnny and his mom had a very good relationship, but she seemed to be a little exasperated with Johnny of late. Would she see this as a good idea? After all, Johnny hadn't exactly been holding up his end of the bargain in the good boy department lately. Johnny concluded his mom was the best route if for no other reason than it would give him a chance to prove to her he could be more responsible. Besides, if the lemonade stand worked as well as he hoped, he wouldn't have to ask her for money all the time, and he knew she would like to hear that.

As Johnny walked into his house through the kitchen door, he immediately ran into his mom. She was getting supper ready, and she was alone. There wouldn't be a better time than now to tell her his plan.

"How was your afternoon over at Mr. C.'s? You sure were gone a long time. You must have gone for a boat ride," said Lou, quizzing Johnny as she sliced tomatoes.

"Well actually, we didn't go for a boat ride, but I did get to see the Titanic," Johnny answered. "Mr. C. unveiled a big one today, and after that we just went inside and talked for a while."

"Yeah, well what did you talk about? It must have been important; you were over there all afternoon," Lou said as she began to slice the onions.

Unknowingly, Johnny's mom had just swung the door wide open for Johnny to make his sales pitch.

Here went nothing.

Over the next few minutes, Johnny told his mom about everything he and Mr. C. had talked about that afternoon. Lou stayed busy slicing while Johnny spilled his guts for the second time that day—the Sunday School lesson of reaping what you sow, his lack of money and why, the three-legged business stool, and his idea of starting a lemonade stand. Johnny didn't leave anything out.

When Johnny finished, Lou turned around and started crying. Johnny didn't know what to say.

"It's OK, Johnny. It's just the onions," Lou said, laughing and crying simultaneously.

What she said next made Johnny's day.

"Well, what are you going to do about this new business idea of yours?" she said as if to put her stamp of approval on the whole thing as she piled all the sliced vegetables in the salad bowl.

"Well," said Johnny slowly, "I was kind of hoping you could help me get started. I mean I think I know what to do next, but I don't have everything I need to get going, and…"

"How much money do you think you'll need?" Lou interrupted, knowing exactly where Johnny was headed with this conversation.

"I'll pay you back, Mom, I promise," Johnny said before realizing how empty those words must have sounded to his mother who had heard that before on several occasions. "Besides, I don't think I will need very much money to get started. Mr. C. helped me understand how to use the capital I already have, and I just need you to help me get it all together."

Lou liked the sound of what she was hearing. It sounded like Johnny was really being serious about this whole lemonade stand business. She really liked the thought of Johnny being thrifty and using what he could to make it happen.

But she also knew sincerity didn't necessarily mean Johnny would follow through with his promises. Lou had been down this road before, and if she was going down it again, she wanted Johnny to have some skin in the game.

"OK, Johnny. I'm in," Lou said, "but with two conditions."

"What's that, Mom?" Johnny asked nervously.

"First, you have to have some skin in the game," Lou said very seriously.

"What do you mean?" Johnny asked, puzzled by the question.

"I mean you have to have something of value that you put into the business other than your own hard work. You see, Johnny, if I put in money to get you started and the business fails, then I am the only one who has lost anything of value. But if we both have money or something valuable invested, then we both have skin in the game. That will make both of us work to make it succeed because neither of us will want to lose our investment. Does that make sense?" Lou asked, trying to get her point across.

Johnny immediately understood his mom's point. Now he had to figure out what he could put into his business that would qualify as "skin in the game." He didn't have any cash, so this was going to require some thinking.

No sooner had that thought crossed his mind than he figured out what he had of value that would give him skin in the game."

"I know what I can invest," Johnny said, as serious as he had ever been before. "I have got ten Frank's Batting Cage tokens that can be used for anything in his store. He has outdoor chairs and umbrellas. I know we are going to need some of that kind of stuff to make a good lemonade stand."

Batting cage tokens were as good as gold. Lou knew that if Johnny was willing to use tokens from his favorite store to help with startup costs, then he was dead serious about making this work.

She agreed that would qualify as "skin in the game."

Now that the first condition had been solved, Johnny asked, "What's number two?"

"As an investor in your company, I get all the free lemonade I want," Lou said as she gave Johnny a big hug.

Johnny was on cloud nine. He was starting a business, and he had just landed his first investor. Even though it was only his mom, it may as well have been Warren Buffett. She was a believer.

"Now help me get this icing on your dad's birthday cake and try to get all forty-five candles in that thing, would ya? We are going to surprise him with it tonight after supper even though his birthday's not until tomorrow," Lou said, directing Johnny where to stick the candles. "We will work on your business plan tomorrow night when you get home from baseball practice."

"Thanks, Mom, I really appreciate what you're doing," Johnny said gratefully, "and thanks for the new Basebusters too."

As Lou finished decorating the three-layer yellow cake with chocolate icing, she could not help but feel good that Johnny seemed to be maturing before her very eyes. She wasn't sure how long this new, responsible, grateful, and visionary season would last, but she was going to enjoy it while it did.

CHAPTER 7
PLAN, PLAN, PLAN

"Great catch, Johnny!" yelled Coach Hill as Johnny tracked down a long fly ball off Jimmy's bat in deep center field. "Head to the batter's box; you're up next."

"You robbed me," howled Jimmy as they passed by each other as Johnny came in for his turn at batting practice.

"You ain't seen nothing yet! Wait 'til I hit a homer over your head in a minute," Johnny said cockily as he loosened up with his bat. Sure enough, on the third pitch from Coach Hill, Johnny connected squarely on a fastball and sent it right over Jimmy's head in deep left field for a homer. The whole team hollered the usual "ding uh" as Johnny circled the bases in his new Basebusters while high-fiving everybody on the team. If Johnny could hit this well when the season got underway in a couple of weeks, the Coyotes were going to have a great year.

Johnny's confidence was soaring. He had just hit the first homer of the year in team practice, and in an hour, he was going to be putting together a "business plan" with his mom. How good was that?

When practice was over, Jimmy and Tony asked Johnny if he wanted to go with them down to Frank's Batting Cage for some extra hitting. Johnny wanted to go, but he knew he had told his mom he would come straight home to work on the plan. Johnny didn't want to tell Jimmy and Tony about the lemonade stand just yet. He wanted to have it a little further along before he let that cat out of the bag.

"Maybe tomorrow," Johnny said. "I've gotta go home and help my mom with a project."

"What kind of project?" Tony shot back, sarcastically.

"Just a little something we're working on together," Johnny told Tony, who was obviously not satisfied that Johnny's project was more important than hitting baseballs at Frank's.

"Hey, Johnny, don't forget about us going back to Castle Mountain Saturday night, and don't forget that it will cost $20," Jimmy reminded Johnny as they all climbed on their bikes.

"Yeah, yeah, I'm in this time," Johnny said loudly as he tied his Basebusters over the handlebars. "I will see you guys tomorrow."

Johnny couldn't help but think about how well the day had gone. Between the home run and business plans, he felt like he was floating on the clouds.

The bike ride home from the practice field usually took about ten minutes. Johnny was riding so fast, he was probably going to cut the trip in half. He was flying around corners and passing everything in sight at breakneck speed.

Johnny had never been so motivated in all his life. As he flew home, his mind raced with thoughts on how to get his business going and how many customers he would have on day one. As he thought about how much money he was going to make on his first day, he lost track of where he was at on South Canal Street and went right through the four-way stop without looking.

The sudden loud noise of a big truck horn shook him back to his senses. Mr. Stroud, the truck driver for his dad's hardware store, was out making deliveries and had alertly seen Johnny speed through the stop sign without looking. Johnny waved sheepishly to Stroud and yelled sorry.

He paid attention the rest of the way home.

As he cruised into the front yard, Bets was sitting on the front porch with the phone stuck to her ear. "You're home early," she said without even so much as interrupting her conversation with VJ.

"Where is Mom?" Johnny asked smartly as he walked by Bets on the porch.

"How would I know?" Bets shot back without even hesitating.

Johnny started to turn around and engage Bets in this verbal tit-for-tat, but something inside of him just kept him moving forward and into the house. He just didn't have time to argue with Bets over nothing.

"Mom!" Johnny yelled as he swung open the door. "I'm home."

"I am in the kitchen," came the voice he was hoping to hear.

Johnny was so excited, he headed straight there without even thinking to put his things away first. "OK, where do we start?" Johnny asked as he dropped his equipment bag on the kitchen floor and sat down at the kitchen table.

When the equipment bag hit the floor, Lou spun around from the kitchen counter, and what happened next almost doomed the entire evening of business planning. Her eyes lit up like fire when she saw Johnny had tracked mud in with him from the baseball field.

"Johnny Mac Williams, you get that filthy, stinkin' bag out of my clean kitchen this minute! I have spent all day cleaning this house, and now look at what you have done. Look at you! You are dirty, and your shoes are muddy. Put that stuff where it belongs right now, and get your butt upstairs and get a shower!" Johnny had definitely made Lou mad.

His eagerness to get started with his business had caused him to have a temporary lapse in remembering and obeying Lou's number one house rule. Don't ever bring unnecessary dirt into the house.

Johnny, immediately sensing his huge mistake, spoke the only four words that could make this situation any better. "Yes ma'am, I'm sorry," he said and quickly got out the back door before he did any more damage. He put the equipment bag and Basebusters in the garage and headed upstairs to clean up before reintroducing himself to the kitchen table.

Ten minutes later, Johnny emerged. "Much better," Lou said as Johnny plopped down at the kitchen table again, now with a fresh set of clothes, a clean face, and a notebook.

"Show me what you have so far," Lou said as she settled into a chair beside Johnny. He wanted to show his mom that he was capable of creating a good plan. Earlier in the day, he had written down Mr. C.'s three-legged stool business model and how it could work for his lemonade stand. Even though his plan was simple, Lou was impressed that he had actually written something down that seemed to make good sense. It showed her that Johnny was taking this whole business idea very seriously.

"Well, we need to start with our product, which is going to be lemonade. Miss Darlene recommended I use three cups of sugar per gallon and six real lemons along with some lemonade powder," Johnny said proudly as if he owned the exclusive rights to a special recipe. "Do you think that sounds good?" he asked.

Lou couldn't help but smile, thinking of how sweet Johnny's "special recipe" lemonade was going to taste with three cups of sugar per gallon. She wasn't about to offer recipe advice that would change Miss Darlene's recommendation.

"Yes, very good. Have you thought about how you are going to serve it?"

"Yep," Johnny said quickly, "in the twelve-ounce paper cups that we had left over from Dad's birthday party last night if you will let me use them. There are 110 left in the box."

"That's smart. I like your thinking, Johnny. Now, how are you going to keep the lemonade cold?" Lou asked.

"I was thinking I would fill our cooler with ice from the machine at Dad's store and put some in each cup before filling it with lemonade."

Lou was beginning to be impressed with Johnny's thoughtfulness. He seemed to have a pretty good grip on what it took to put together a good glass of cold lemonade.

"I like the fact you have thought about using what we have on hand, but have you considered how much the sugar and lemons and powder are going to cost and how much you are going to need?"

Johnny was one step ahead of his mom. After school and before baseball practice, he had ridden his bike to Shockley's Grocery and had written down the prices of all three items. Lemons were $2 per dozen. A five-pound bag of sugar was $2, and a sixteen-ounce jar of lemonade powder was $4.

Lou was stunned. She had never seen Johnny this responsible before. She leaned back in her chair and just looked at him. Something good was happening before her very eyes, and she was just soaking it in. She had believed up until that moment that she was going to have to hold Johnny's hand as he got his new venture off the ground. Now she knew otherwise; Johnny was on top of everything. He had even figured out how many packs of each item he was going to need to make a hundred cups of lemonade.

By Johnny's count, each cup should cost him about 20 cents. If he charged $1 and sold a hundred cups, he would make $80.

She just let Johnny keep going with his plan, and he moved right into the things he was going to need to get his product to market. Mr. C. had called this second leg "capital."

Johnny had his list: Two tables. One chair. One umbrella. One tablecloth. Two signs. Some money to make change. Napkins. A small trash can.

As good as his plan was, Lou knew that for it to be successful, Johnny would need to be in a location that had some people traffic. "Have you thought about where you want to put it?" she asked.

"Well, I was thinking about asking Mr. Morgan if I could set up on the sidewalk in front of the bank. Do you think he would let me?"

Lou knew that would be a great location. The bank was right downtown on Main Street, and there would be plenty of traffic there on Saturday. "That's a great spot, Johnny, if you can get Mr. Morgan to say yes. You should go by and see him tomorrow and ask him. What's your backup plan if he says no?"

"I'm sure Dad would let me set up down at the hardware store, but there is just not much room on the front sidewalk, and it's a full block off Main Street," Johnny replied.

Lou liked his plan and was totally convinced that Johnny was going to be successful. "OK," she said, "you had me at Shockley's. I'm in for a $20 investment."

As Lou shooed him away from the table so she could get supper ready, Billy got home from the hardware store, and Johnny got to tell his plan all over again. Supper was fun because Johnny couldn't stop talking about his business and what he was going to do with the profits. Even Bets seemed nicer.

In five days, Johnny was going to be a businessman.

CHAPTER 8
OPENING DAY

The week flew by.

Johnny had met with Mr. Morgan on Tuesday in between school and baseball practice, and Mr. Morgan had said yes. He just wanted to make sure Johnny didn't pressure anyone into buying the lemonade. Johnny had secured a great location.

He had met with Mr. C. again on Wednesday to explain his plan and make sure he was on the right track. Mr. C. was extremely excited and told Johnny he wanted to be one of his first customers. He assured Johnny that he had a good plan and that he was going to be very successful.

On Thursday night, Johnny and Lou worked on the signs for the lemonade stand together at the kitchen table. Johnny didn't know how much fun work could be until now. Something was different about this work. It just didn't feel like work.

On Friday afternoon at baseball practice, Johnny finally told Jimmy and Tony what was going on and why he had been so elusive all week. Tony was relieved. He had thought Johnny had gotten into some trouble at home and was on some kind of bad restriction. Jimmy just wanted to know if he was going to get free lemonade, to which Johnny replied, "Drop dead."

When he got home from practice, Johnny and Lou headed straight to Shockley's to get the stuff. Both of them were laughing and smiling as they made their way through the store. Picking out the lemons was especially fun. Miss Darlene had not specified what size lemons to get, and Shockley's had both small and large.

Johnny had to make his first major business decision, and he went with the large lemons. He wanted his first day to be memorable, and he just felt like large lemons would be better for his customers.

They stopped by the hardware store on the way home and filled the cooler with ice. When they got home from Shockley's, Lou helped Johnny mix the lemonade into five jugs. Billy volunteered to be the official taste tester, and after a few swigs, he declared it the "world's best homemade lemonade." Even Bets said it was good.

Johnny loaded up the van that evening with all the supplies and items he was going to need for the next morning. He checked his list three times and went back inside the house to do the hardest thing any new business owner had to face—the anxious wait for opening day.

The plan was simple. They would leave the house at eight o'clock in the morning for the short ride into downtown to set up. The bank and most of the other businesses opened at nine o'clock, so there would be plenty of time to get everything in place and ready to go.

At about ten minutes after eight, Lou pulled the van up to the bank sidewalk, and they unloaded all the materials and the lemonade. After they unloaded, she moved the car to a nearby parking place and returned to help Johnny get set up.

As they were setting up the table and taping the signs onto the umbrella, Mr. Jackson, the local barber, stopped by, wished Johnny well, and told him he would send him some customers after he finished cutting their hair. Johnny thanked him, and as Mr. Jackson left going to open his shop, Miss Cindy, who owned Schaub's Decorations and Flowers, stopped by to see what the new business was going to be selling.

At about eight forty-five, Johnny and Lou had finished setting up the lemonade stand. More than ten business owners had already stopped by to wish Johnny well, and each had promised to come buy some lemonade and to send their customers over as well.

Johnny was almost feeling giddy over all the buzz his new stand was generating.

At five minutes until nine, Lou got Johnny to stand still long enough to get a great picture of him pouring the first cup for Mr. Morgan. Johnny gave it to Mr. Morgan for free as a thank you for letting him set up on the bank sidewalk.

Mr. Morgan wished Johnny well, reminded him about his "no pressure" pledge, and then went back inside the bank.

After the picture, Lou gave Johnny a big hug and told him how proud she was. "I will be back around nine thirty. I need to go run some errands," she said.

"Thanks for all your help, Mom. I think we are going to do really good today," Johnny said as he was already imagining selling out of lemonade on his first day.

With all the well-wishers who had come by the stand, most of the butterflies in Johnny's stomach were already gone, and now it was show time.

The big moment had arrived.

Right on time, at exactly nine o'clock, Mr. C. walked up to the stand. "Are you open for business Johnny?" beamed Mr. C.

"I sure am," Johnny said with a huge smile.

"Pour me a big one, Johnny," Mr. C. said heartily as he watched with a mentor's pride as Johnny operated his new business.

Mr. C. pulled out his wallet and handed Johnny his first dollar as Johnny passed the lemonade.

"This is good stuff. I could swear I have had this before. Where did you get the recipe?" Mr. C. said, smiling.

Mr. C. hung around for a couple of minutes, sipping on his lemonade while he and Johnny shared some more laughs and business start-up stories. Johnny thanked Mr. C. for his inspiration and for all his encouragement.

Mr. C. quickly returned the accolades to Johnny and told him how inspiring it was to see one of his students do something so grand as to start a business from scratch.

"I will bring Darlene by in a couple of hours after she finishes up at Bookie's Beauty Shop," he said as he headed towards his car.

Nobody knew exactly how Bookie got her name, but all the women in town went to her for their hairdos. For an extra dollar, she would mysteriously tell her customers what the winning bingo number was going to be at the monthly Garden Club meeting. She hadn't missed a number in years.

As Mr. C. backed out of his parking spot, Johnny waved good-bye and then looked down at the "Washington" he was still holding in his hand. It was the first dollar his business had made, and he knew this was a special moment. All kinds of thoughts started dancing through his head about how much money he was going to make.

This was going to be easy.

CHAPTER 9
DISASTER

Johnny had been so busy setting up the stand and taking pictures with Mr. Morgan and serving his first customer that he hadn't noticed what was ominously gathering in the sky.

This was spring, and springtime in Belleville could mean quickly developing brutal storms.

Johnny could not believe what he was now feeling and seeing. The wind was becoming brisk, and the sky had definitely started turning gray.

All of his good fortune was suddenly at risk.

This couldn't happen—not on opening day.

Suddenly and without any more warning, lightning flashed across the sky, and thunder rattled overhead.

"Oh no," Johnny gasped, as he tried to think through what he would do if the storm unleashed on him.

He had thought of everything in his plan. He had a great product. He had capital and a great location, and customers were telling him they were coming to buy his lemonade.

He just hadn't thought about things that were beyond his control—like the weather.

No sooner had he finished that thought than the bottom fell out and the winds howled. The first gust blew the cups off the table and into the street. As he ran after the cups and tried to save them, the second gust was the killer.

The umbrella started leaning, and before Johnny could grab it, it crashed into the lemonade and knocked over all five gallons onto the sidewalk.

Johnny tried desperately to get the jugs upright and save some of the lemonade, but it was useless. The wind was blowing so fast and the rain was falling so hard, the whole lemonade stand was being torn apart. The paper tablecloth had virtually disintegrated, and the two signs were airborne and flying down the street. The money box had fallen off the table, and quarters were rolling everywhere.

Lou had been at the cleaners picking up one of Billy's Sunday suits and had seen the storm coming. She had jumped into her van and tried to get back to the stand to help, but she got there too late. She pulled up to the curb and rolled the window down. "Johnny, get in!" she yelled, barely audible as the wind and the rain were now vicious in their deluge.

Johnny dashed for the van and got in the front seat as quickly as he could. When he closed the door, he slumped down into the seat and just groaned.

"I'm so sorry, Johnny, I'm so sorry," his mom kept repeating trying to soothe his pain. "I know how much this meant to you, and I'm just so sorry. Maybe it will stop soon."

Lou's wish didn't come true.

They just sat there in silence for thirty minutes while the torrential rains just completely battered Johnny's Lemonade Stand.

As Johnny just stared out the van window, all he could see was disaster. The carnage was everywhere.

The umbrella was upside down and broken. All the cups had washed away. Johnny could see only one jug left under the table, and it was turned over. The cloth pop-up chair had been blown down the sidewalk and into a mud puddle. The trash can was nowhere to be seen.

All was lost.

When the rain finally reduced itself to a drizzle, Johnny and Lou gathered what remained of a once promising business venture and solemnly loaded everything into the van.

Lou tried to cheer Johnny up and make it better, but nothing she said could stop the pain Johnny felt.

He was wavering somewhere between very sick and dead, and this misery wasn't going to be eased because of his mom's encouragement—no matter how hard she tried.

He hadn't felt this bad since Big Mel had hit him in the kidney with a fastball during the opening day game last season.

Johnny's mom could be a bulldog, and she sensed her role was to keep encouraging Johnny in the middle of this crisis. "The sun is going to come up tomorrow, Johnny. Keep your head up. We can do this again," she said as they finally pulled into their driveway at 101 South Canal Street.

As Johnny opened the van door, Bets appeared from the garage and instantly knew by the look on Johnny's face that something had gone wrong.

"Don't even ask," Johnny growled as he brushed by her and headed into the house.

"What happened?" Bets asked Lou as she got out of the van.

"It was awful, Bets, just awful. Everything was going so well at first. Johnny had gotten the stand all set up, and people were stopping by, and I took his picture with Mr. Morgan getting the first cup. I told him I had to run some errands, and then I headed over to Mary Jean's Cleaners to get your dad's suit. Just as I drove up, it started getting very dark. I knew this storm was going to be trouble because it just came out of nowhere. I turned around and headed back, but by the time I got back to the bank it was raining cats and dogs. Johnny was trying to save what he could, but it was too late. The umbrella got blown over, and it knocked over the lemonade. Everything just got destroyed. It was just awful, Bets."

Bets, who was never without a word, was speechless.

She helped her mom unload the ice cooler, and both of them headed inside to check on Johnny.

They found him at the kitchen table, talking to somebody on the phone. He would occasionally mumble "yeah" or "I know," but neither Bets nor Lou could figure out who he was talking with. It didn't appear to be Billy or Mr. C. Finally, the conversation ended with Johnny saying, "I promise, I will," and almost appearing to smile.

"Who was that?" Lou asked.

"It was Mr. Jackson," Johnny replied softly.

"Mr. Jackson, the barber?"

"Yes."

"What did he want?"

"He said he wanted his glass of lemonade, and he was going to hold my sign hostage until I promised to set my stand up again and give it another go. The sign blew in his front door when the storm hit, and he saw the whole stand get blown to bits."

"Well, is the sign useable?" Lou said, trying to be cheery.

"Yeah, he says it's in pretty good shape. Do we have anything to eat? I'm starving."

Lou knew this was a good sign. When fourteen-year-old boys are hungry, things are normal. She grabbed some cookies that were cooling on top of the stove and slid the whole pan in front of Johnny. Sensing the trauma was easing, she asked him what else Mr. Jackson had said as they were on the phone for a while.

"He was just telling me about his first day in business. He said he only had one customer all day, and he was so nervous that he accidentally cut the man's ear. He felt so bad; he only charged him a dollar."

Johnny suddenly realized he too had made a dollar on his first day in business. He reached into his pocket and pulled out the wet, crumbled-up one-dollar bill that Mr. C. had used to pay for his lemonade. George Washington never looked so good.

It was not much, but it was better than nothing.

"Here, Mom, this is yours," Johnny said as he pushed the dollar bill across the table to Lou. "Now I only owe you $19 more. If you will still help me, I think I am going to take Mr. Jackson's advice and give it another go. Besides, I've got skin in this game, and next Saturday, we are going to be ready for anything. Johnny's Lemonade Stand is still open for business."

Lou was amazed at Johnny's resilience. She felt tears begin to well up in her eyes just thinking about what Johnny had just gone through. She caught herself before the tears began to roll and knew she couldn't get wobbly in front of Johnny.

"You're on!" she said as she and Johnny smiled and laughed for the first time since the great storm. "Next Saturday is going to be a great day, Johnny, I just know it is."

After he finished eating his cookies, Johnny headed outside to clean out the van and see what was left that might be useable for next week.

Lou just sat at the table, thinking about how proud she was of Johnny Mac Williams. While Johnny's first day in business was full of huge losses and no profits, Lou had learned something about her son that was much bigger than money.

Johnny Mac Williams was no quitter.

He had been knocked down, but he had gotten back up. Grandpa would be proud of this fighter.

CHAPTER 10
ROCK STAR

"Johnny! Johnny Mac Williams! It's your turn. Let's go," Miss Evans said loudly, trying to get Johnny's attention.

It was only Tuesday, and the week had slowed to a crawl. As Johnny sat in math class, he had let his mind wander ahead to Saturday and the re-opening of his lemonade stand. Johnny had so much to do before Saturday morning to be ready.

As he passed by Jimmy's and Tony's desks on his way to the front of the class, they goosed him in the side and laughed that he had been caught daydreaming by Miss Evans.

Miss Evans hated it when kids didn't pay attention, and Johnny knew his punishment was going to be a very hard math problem. Every Tuesday each kid had to go up to the chalkboard and complete a math equation in front of the whole class. Miss Evans would put all the problems on the board, and each student could choose which one they wanted to solve. The easy problems always got chosen early in the process.

The class would always go to the board in alphabetical order, and this was one instance when having the last name Williams wasn't a good thing.

Johnny was pretty good at math, though, and he wasn't too concerned about being able to solve any of the problems that were left on the chalkboard.

As he rounded the front row desk where Susie Brewster sat, he headed toward the far end of the chalkboard to answer the next-to-last problem on the board, "What is the square root of 529?"

Right before he picked up the chalk to begin explaining the square root of 529, Miss Evans stopped him.

"Johnny, I think I want you to do something different," Miss Evans said matter-of-factly.

This wasn't going to be good, Johnny thought to himself. The price for not paying attention was about to be paid.

"I want you to show the class in detail how much profit is in a glass of lemonade if the customers pay a dollar each and you sell fifty glasses."

Johnny couldn't believe what he had just heard. He was expecting the worst math problem imaginable. He was sure he was going to get a mind bender that was going to stump him in front of the class and be a solid reminder to pay attention in the future.

Johnny relaxed and started to smile. Miss Evans just nodded in an approving kind of way that only a teacher can do. Somehow, she had found out he was in the lemonade business.

"Well, it's actually pretty simple," Johnny said as he began to put numbers up on the chalkboard and explain to the class how he figured the profit on each glass of lemonade. Step-by-step, Johnny showed each layer of cost involved in getting a glass of lemonade in the hands of a customer. As he went through the cost of each ingredient, he couldn't help but remember how he had done the same thing for his mom at their kitchen table. Explaining his business model for the second time came easily, and Johnny relaxed and had fun with the spontaneous presentation.

When he was finished, Miss Evans walked over to the chalkboard where Johnny's profit equation was now on display. She showed the class where Johnny had used addition, subtraction, division, and multiplication in explaining how to determine the profit.

Miss Evans then told the class that she had heard via word of mouth that Johnny's Lemonade Stand had the best lemonade in Belleville and they should give it a try.

He had only sold one glass, and already everybody seemed to know about his lemonade stand.

Johnny felt like a rock star.

Miss Evans thanked Johnny for his business lesson, and since class was about to end, she laid out the homework plan for the rest of the week. Groans came from all four corners of the room as Miss Evans's goodwill and mercy had come to an end.

As he rounded the corner at Susie's desk on the way back to his desk, Susie motioned to Johnny and handed him a note on pink paper that she had neatly folded. Johnny stuffed the note in his pocket and reached his desk just as the bell rang and class was over.

"Hey, Johnny, hurry up, we got a practice game today against the Blue Jays," Jimmy said as he passed by Johnny, who was still putting his books in his backpack.

"You mean the Buzzards," Tony hooted as he brought up the rear of the group hurrying to get out the classroom door before Miss Evans could assign any more homework.

"Why did we schedule a practice game with the Buzzards? What was Coach Hill thinking? You know what this means Tony?" Johnny asked as he slung his backpack over his shoulder.

"Yeah, I know what it means," Tony replied with fear in his voice. "It means Big Mel is gonna be pitching for the

Buzzards. He's wilder than a tazmo. I bet he hits ten batters today with his fastball."

"I ain't scared!" Jimmy said emphatically.

Both Tony and Johnny laughed out loud.
"That's because you're too chicken to even get close to the plate when he's pitching. You got no chance of getting hit, Jimmy, and you definitely got no chance of getting a hit that far from the plate," Tony laughed as he slammed Jimmy.

"Yeah, you just watch today," Jimmy yelled back, trying to defend his batting tactics against Big Mel as they got on their bikes and headed to the baseball field.

It was no use. Tony and Johnny were still laughing at Jimmy's story, and until Jimmy got a hit off Big Mel, they were gonna keep on laughing.

As they cruised up to the field, Coach Hill was already throwing some warm-up pitches, and everybody was getting ready for the practice game. Several parents lined up along the fence to watch Big Mel's first outing of the year. Big Mel was a star around Belleville, and everybody liked to see him pitch even if it was just a practice game.

Johnny overheard one parent tell another that Big Mel was more popular in Belleville than the sheriff.

Johnny, Jimmy, and Tony had to walk past the Blue Jay's bullpen to get to their side of the field. As they got close to the bullpen, they could hear Big Mel's fastball hitting the catcher's mitt. Big Mel was warming up, and he was throwing hard—real hard.

"What's up, Melvin? I'm thinking about taking your buzzard breath deep today," Johnny said sarcastically as he walked by the bullpen, knowing full well that calling Big Mel by his real name would get under his skin. Nobody ever called Big Mel by his real name. Nobody but Johnny.

"Nothing much, yard dog. Why don't you take your two little puppies and get off our side of the field," a red-faced Big Mel shot back.

Big Mel was somewhat of a freak of nature. He was fourteen, and the rumor was his fastball was now up to ninety miles per hour.

Johnny just smiled as they walked on by, knowing he had just got inside Big Mel's head. This was gonna be fun. Johnny and Big Mel had played against each other for seven years at every stage of Dixie baseball, and every year the rivalry had gotten more intense.

Big Mel's team had won the city championship the previous season, and Johnny was ready to get the trophy back for the Coyotes where it belonged.

Coach Hill gathered up the Coyotes after a few warm up tosses and gave his usual speech. Good pitching. No errors. Get on base. Score some runs. Play hard all seven innings. The speech never changed.

As the game got underway, it was very clear this one was going to be a pitcher's duel. Big Mel was throwing for the Blue Jays, and Vinny, who was Tony's cousin, was throwing for the Coyotes. Both were pitching a great game even though they had entirely different styles. Going into the seventh inning, both were pitching a shutout.

Big Mel was overpowering. His fastball was just not hittable. Through six innings, he had struck out twelve, only walked two, and had not even hit a single batter. The Blue Jays yelled "yard dog!" every time Big Mel struck out a Coyote.

Vince had three pitches—slow curve ball, really slow curve ball, and super slow curve ball. Every time he got a strikeout, the Coyotes would yell "dead buzzard!" in unison.

In the top of the seventh, the Blue Jays finally strung together three hits off Vince and pushed a run across for a 1–0 lead heading into the bottom of the inning. Tony had made a great throw from the outfield to get the last out at home plate, or the Buzzards would have scored again.

Vince was the leadoff batter for the Coyotes in the bottom of the seventh inning. Three pitches later, Vince had struck out. Big Mel was on fire.

With one out, the Coyotes just had to get a man on base if they had any chance. Tony was the next batter, and Coach Hill gave him the bunt sign as he was getting ready to hit. On the very next pitch, Big Mel's control finally came unglued, and he hit Tony right in the stomach with a blazing fastball. The whole crowd swooned, and Tony fell to the ground, moaning and gasping for air.

After a couple of minutes, Tony got up, stared at Big Mel, and trotted down to first base.

The Coyotes started cheering for Tony. He had taken one for the team, and now they had a man on base.

With one out and a man on base, it was now Jimmy's turn to bat. After watching Tony get stung, Jimmy's knees were visibly shaking. Coach Hill yelled for Jimmy to get tighter in the batter's box, but there was no way Jimmy was getting close to that ninety-mile-per-hour fastball. Jimmy was at least three feet from the plate and didn't come close to hitting any of the pitches Big Mel threw. To Jimmy's credit, he at least went down swinging even though he did have his eyes closed on three straight pitches.

The Coyotes' last hope was now down to the bat of Johnny Mac Williams.

Johnny was very calm. Unlike Jimmy, Big Mel's fastball had never intimidated Johnny. He knew the key to getting a hit off Big Mel was to get close to the plate and get a hit early in the pitch count before Big Mel had you reeling on the ropes. Big Mel had struck Johnny out in the first inning. In the fourth inning, Johnny had flied-out to the center fielder.

Even though Big Mel had struck him out earlier, he felt good.

On the first pitch, Big Mel threw a fastball right under Johnny's chin. Johnny wheeled around just in the nick of time and hit the dirt to avoid a possible broken jaw. When he got up, Big Mel was standing nearby and told Johnny, "If you're scared, call the police, yard dog."

Johnny asked the umpire for time and stepped out of the batter's box to regain his senses.

Jimmy, who Big Mel had humiliated just a few minutes earlier, decided it was time to take action. He stood up in the dugout and told all the Coyotes to follow his lead.

As Big Mel got back to the pitcher's mound, all of the Coyotes in the dugout begin to yell.

"MELVIN! MELVIN! MELVIN!"

Johnny knew Jimmy was taking a big chance and that the next time Jimmy faced Big Mel he was going to get a fastball right at his gut, but this was working brilliantly. Big Mel's face was turning redder by the second. He got so discombobulated that the next pitch landed in the dirt five feet in front of the plate. Jimmy's plan was working.

Jimmy and the Coyotes started yelling louder.

"MELVIN! MELVIN! MELVIN!"

Big Mel was fuming. They were getting under his skin, and he lost focus. He knew Johnny was a good hitter, but he thought he could strike him out just throwing a screamer right down the middle of the plate.

Big mistake.

Johnny knew it was gone when he hit it. The Blue Jays' center fielder watched it sail high over his head and over the fence—a game-ending two-run homer off Big Mel.

Jimmy and all the Coyotes came flying out of the dugout.

Tony was just a-hollering as he rounded the bases in front of his team, and Coach Hill was jumping up and down as Johnny rounded third base, headed home.

Big Mel was still standing on the mound in disbelief; he had just given up a two-run homer that cost the Blue Jays the game.

You would have thought the Coyotes had just won the World Series.

When Johnny crossed home plate, the whole team mobbed him with joy.

Even though this game was just a practice game, the Coyotes knew all along that beating the "Buzzards" was huge. They were the toughest competition in the league, and Big Mel was their five-star unbeatable pitcher.

The Coyotes had sent a message.

There was a new sheriff in town.

His name was Johnny Mac Williams.

CHAPTER 11
LIFE IS GOOD

"I heard you hit the game-winning homer in the practice game today against Big Mel!" Billy said as Lou passed more potatoes around the supper table.

"Yeah, everybody was hooting and hollering. We play the Buzzards again in two weeks on opening day, and I'm sure Big Mel will be ready for me. Are you gonna be able to come?" Johnny said as he finished off the potatoes.

"Sure am," Billy replied, "and I want to see another homer off the king buzzard." Johnny laughed at the thought of Big Mel's new nickname. Jimmy and Tony were gonna like that one.

As Johnny got up to leave the supper table, Bets noticed a pink paper sticking out of his pocket. She couldn't help herself. "What's your love letter say?"

"What are you talking about, Bets?"

"I am talking about that little pink note sticking out of your pocket. Sounds like you're trying to hide something to me. So, who's the girl?"

Up until that moment, Johnny had completely forgotten Susie Brewster had given him the note earlier that day in Miss Evans's math class. He had no idea what it said, but he certainly wasn't going to read it in front of Bets.

"You got a girl now, Johnny?" Billy asked joining the ribbing Bets had begun. "Seems to me you got enough on your plate with a lemonade stand and trying to help the Coyotes win a championship. Are you sure you got time to be chasing a girl?"

This pink note discovery had suddenly gotten way out of hand. Johnny, now embarrassed at what it might say, finished pulling the note out of his pocket. He turned his back to the table while he quickly unfolded the note and read it to himself for the first time.

"It's nothing," reported Johnny.

"Oh really," Bets said snidely. "Then tell us what it says!"

Johnny knew he had two paths to choose from in how he responded to Bets. On the one hand, he could choose to be coy and just let Bets keep wondering what the note said. He liked the idea of getting under Bets's skin and letting her wallow in her desire to know what the note said. This path also had a big downside. What if Bets told her friends he was getting secret notes from some unknown girlfriend? He could hear that rumor mill churning and somehow getting back to the Coyotes. All the guys would be making fun of him.

The other path was to just read the note out loud and solve the mystery once and for all.

Johnny chose to read the note. "I enjoyed hearing about your lemonade stand. If you need some help, just let me know. Thanks, Susie Brewster."

"Happy now, Bets? I told you it was nothing," Johnny said, laughing at the spurned look on Bets's face. She obviously had been hoping for something a bit more juicy than an offer to help with Johnny's lemonade stand.

Lou, amused by the whole exchange, changed the subject from girls to lemonade and asked Johnny if he was ready to go for the re-opening coming up on Saturday.

Johnny assured Lou he was ready. The day before, he had gone down to the hardware store and borrowed two concrete blocks to use as anchors to hold the umbrella in the event of another storm. He had also made another list of items he would need to get from Shockley's.

Johnny and Lou agreed to go to Shockley's Thursday after baseball practice and get the ingredients for another batch of lemonade. He told his mom he was keeping a tab of how much she was investing and that she would be the first one paid. Lou said OK to the new plan and sent Johnny off to finish his math homework and take a shower.

After what seemed like an endless week of baseball practice, homework, and lemonade stand preparations, Saturday morning finally arrived.

Both he and Lou had watched The Weather Channel one last time before leaving the house, just to be sure. There were no concerns today. The forecast was 100 percent sunshine and a high of eighty degrees. Their favorite weatherman, Jimbo Canatorbe, had definitely hit a home run today.

From making the lemonade to setting up the stand in front of the bank, everything went smoother this time. The experience Johnny had gained a week earlier made setup for week two a breeze.

He was completely ready to go by eight forty-five, and Lou left him to go and run some errands with a promise to keep an eye on the skies just in case the weather went crazy again. He had time to sit down and relax a little before he opened for business at nine. Everything looked great, and Johnny tested the lemonade one more time to make sure Miss Darlene's special formula was ready to go.

He had planned for selling a hundred cups and staying open until three o'clock in the afternoon. By his calculations and estimates, if all went well, he would be able to pay his mom back and still have $60 left over.

Johnny never saw it coming.

He had stepped inside the bank to greet Mr. Morgan just before nine o'clock and thank him again for letting him set up his stand on the sidewalk.

When he emerged from the bank's front door to open for business, he couldn't believe his eyes.

There was a line of eight to ten people already waiting to get a cup of lemonade.

Mr. Jackson was in the front. "I have been waiting all week for this, Johnny. I sure am proud of you for sticking it out. By the way, your sign looks great."

Johnny started dipping ice and pouring lemonade as fast as he could. "Thanks Mr. Jackson, I really appreciate your encouragement. I don't know if I would have been here today if you hadn't called me last week."

"I'm next," Miss Bookie said, "and hurry it up. I already have Miss Simpson under the hair dryer, and she wants one too. Give me two glasses."

"Yes ma'am," Johnny said, "and please tell Miss Simpson I am really sorry about the bleach bucket accident."

Miss Bookie laughed and gave Johnny a hug and a kiss on his cheek as she gave him her money then headed back to her beauty shop to tend to hairdressing and bingo.

Johnny kept pouring, and people kept coming. Uncle Ted, Uncle Nathan, and Johnny's dad all came by, as well as Pastor Miller and Mayor Selmon.

By ten thirty when Lou came by to check on him, he had already sold sixty cups and was getting low on ice. He had been so busy, he had to leave the cooler top open, and the ice was melting because of the warm day.

"Mom, it's been crazy. If it stays this busy, I may need you to help."

"What do you need me to do?" Lou said, excited about Johnny's great start.

"We're going to need more lemonade and cups. When you get back, I will pull the cooler around the corner to Dad's store and refill it with ice. Here is some money for the ingredients and the cups," he said as he handed her $20.

Lou left as quickly as she could to go get more lemonade ready.

Johnny got back to pouring cups and making money as the line had grown again.

As Johnny was pouring two cups for Mr. C. and Darlene, Susie Brewster and her mother, Delilah, came out the front door of the bank and walked up to the stand.

"How's it going?" Susie asked.

"Really good," Johnny said as he waved goodbye to Mr. C. and Darlene as they headed to Bookie's and William's Hardware. "If it stays this busy, I may need to take you up on your offer to help me."

Susie jumped all over that opening. "Do you really mean it? I mean, I would be glad to watch your stand for a little while if you need to take a break. What do you think, Mom, can you go to Samson's without me while I help Johnny?"

"Sure honey, I'll be back in about fifteen minutes. I just need to pick up those water hoses for your dad."

Johnny showed Susie how much he wanted her to pour in each cup and where to put the money in his cash box. She started pouring lemonade while Johnny tried to figure out if he was going to have enough ice to last until Lou got back with more lemonade and cups. He quickly decided he was going to run out of ice very soon. He asked Susie if she felt comfortable running the stand by herself while he ran around the corner to refill the cooler with ice.

"Oh sure," she said, and they filled seven more cups with ice to empty the cooler.

Johnny took off to the hardware store, leaving full control of his new business in the hands of Susie Brewster. When he returned in about ten minutes, everything was fine. Susie had sold six cups of lemonade and was smiling from ear to ear, thankful that Johnny had let her help out.

Johnny and Susie chatted and worked together for another five minutes or so before Delilah returned from Samson's Automotive with her husband's water hoses and motioned for Susie to rejoin her in the car.

Johnny offered to pay her $5, but she refused and thanked him instead for letting her help.

As Susie and Delilah were pulling out of the parking lot, Lou was pulling back in with the second wave of lemonade and cups. Johnny helped her unload and restocked his table with plenty of inventory.

It was now eleven thirty in the morning, and he had sold almost a hundred cups of lemonade.

This was just unbelievable. Lou and Johnny were both stunned at how well the day was going.

Lou left to go get Bets and take her and VJ to Brooke's house for a birthday party and told Johnny she would be back around two forty-five to help load up the lemonade stand.

Saturday afternoon saw a steady stream of customers even though it wasn't quite as busy as the morning had been. Several of the guys from the Coyotes stopped by. Jimmy and Tony hung out for about thirty minutes, laughing and talking baseball and telling their Big Mel batting stories.

Jimmy and Tony demanded free refills of their lemonade, and Johnny finally relented on the refills but had to put a cap on Jimmy at two. They made their plans to meet at Castle Mountain later that evening around six o'clock. Johnny was finally going, and he was paying with his own money.

It felt good.

Lou arrived right on time and helped Johnny load up the lemonade stand and the leftovers. When they finished loading, they sat in the front seat of the van while Johnny counted the money.

Lou got misty-eyed as Johnny counted out $165 in cash and then handed her $39—$19 that he owed her for the week one disaster and $20 that he owed her for fronting the money for week two.

Combined with the $20 Johnny had already given Lou out of the cash box to buy more lemonade and cups that morning, he had made and sold 185 cups of lemonade.

He had now paid all his debts and still had $126 left over.

Johnny's Lemonade Stand was a smashing success.

This had been one of the best weeks of Johnny's life.

Miss Evans had made him feel like a rock star in front of the whole class, he had hit a game-winning homer off Big Mel, and he had sold 185 cups of lemonade on his second Saturday in business.

My, oh my, how things had changed in a week's time.
Wow. Life was good.

CHAPTER 12
QUITTING IS NOT AN OPTION

"Johnny, make sure you call Mr. Morgan when you get home from practice. He called again—said he would be home tonight but out of town tomorrow and needed to talk to you. That's the second time this week he has called."

"Yes, Mom, I will," Johnny said politely as he grabbed some cookies and headed out the door for the final practice game against the Bulls before the baseball season officially opened next Tuesday.

It was already Thursday afternoon, and Johnny had been busy all week with three semester tests and baseball practice every afternoon. Not to mention he had already started the planning and preparation for a huge Saturday at the lemonade stand.

The weather was shaping up nicely for Saturday with another eighty-degree day in the forecast and no rain. With a little luck, Johnny felt like he could make a run at 200 cups of lemonade.

The Bulls were no match for the Coyotes, who easily won the practice game 7–2 behind solid pitching from their backup pitcher, Ernie. Johnny played well and had two hits and three RBIs to lead the Coyotes.

After the game, Coach Hill told the team how proud he was to be the leader of the Coyotes and how much he was looking forward to that opening game against the Blue Jays next Tuesday. He told the team to go to Frank's over the weekend if they got a chance and get some batting practice off the fast machine so they would be ready for Big Mel come game time.

When Johnny got home, he headed upstairs to get a shower and completely forgot to call Mr. Morgan.

On Friday afternoon, Johnny and Lou went to Shockley's to get the ingredients, and Johnny loaded the van later that evening with all the lemonade stand supplies. He had developed a routine in mixing the lemonade and loading the van, and each time got a little faster and a little easier.

Johnny's confidence was pretty much on cruise control and definitely flying at a very high altitude. Everything was going his way.

"What did Mr. Morgan want earlier this week?" Lou asked as she backed out of the driveway on Saturday morning, headed to Johnny's spot in front of the bank.

"I forgot to call him back. I'll run into the bank and see him after I get the stand set up."

"Johnny," Lou chided as she shot Johnny a stare that only a mom can give, "you should have called Mr. Morgan back. It may have been important. He called looking for you twice."

"I know. I know. I'm sorry. I just got busy and forgot, Mom. I'll run in the bank first thing when we get there and see what he wanted," Johnny said, trying to appease Lou's anxiety over his forgetfulness.

As they turned the corner at Bookie's onto Main Street, it became obvious why Mr. Morgan had been calling Johnny.

"Oh my gosh! Oh. My. Gosh," Lou said with astonishment.

Johnny was speechless.

Sitting nice and pretty right on the sidewalk in front of the bank was a brand-new lemonade stand.

The sign said it all: "SUSIE'S FRESH PINK LEMONADE."

Everything was pink. The umbrella. The tablecloth. The cups. All pink.

Smoke was pouring out of Lou's ears. The look on her face was pure rage. Johnny had never seen his mom get this mad so fast. They wheeled into a parking spot, and they both jumped out of the van and headed toward the bank. Johnny had a hard time keeping up with Lou. Her feet were hardly touching the ground as she headed straight toward Mr. Morgan, who was coming out of the front door.

"Mr. Morgan, of all the dirty, low-down, rotten things I've ever seen, this takes the cake," Lou said sternly as she approached the Belleville Bank president.

"Now, now, Lou. Just hold on to your horses," Mr. Morgan replied, trying to repel Lou's assault. "I tried to call Johnny twice this week to discuss this, and he never returned my calls. I never said Johnny could have this spot every week. We have other customers just like you, Lou, and they have children who want to have a business too. We can't play favorites."

"And I suppose the fact that Susie is your granddaughter had nothing to do with your decision to replace Johnny, now did it Mr. Morgan!" Lou snarled, getting madder by the second.

Mr. Morgan's face turned beet red as Lou had hit him harder than he expected. "I have a bank to open. I'm sorry it had to be this way, but I tried to call Johnny twice to discuss splitting the time each month with Susie, and he didn't call me back."

Johnny felt like he had just been hit in the gut by a Big Mel fastball.

Mr. Morgan had fired him, and Susie Brewster had stuck him in the back with a knife.

Johnny's eyes shifted to the pink lemonade stand where Susie continued to set up. She would not even look at him. All he could think about was last Saturday when he had let Susie help him. She must have been setting him up all along.

Johnny felt like a gullible fool, and it was an awful feeling.

To make matters worse, he had let his mom down by being irresponsible and not calling Mr. Morgan back. He could have avoided all of this if he had just done what he said he was going to do.

Johnny didn't know for sure what to do next, but he knew quitting wasn't an option.

The last time Big Mel had hit him with a fastball, he had gotten back in the batter's box on his next at bat and gotten a hit.

He figured business was a lot like baseball.

Just get back in the box.

CHAPTER 13
YOU FIND WHAT YOU'RE LOOKING FOR

"Mom, I have an idea," Johnny said as he grabbed her hand and gently pulled her away from her confrontation with Mr. Morgan.

"What kind of an idea? Do you want to set up in front of your dad's hardware store?" Lou asked.

"No, the traffic won't be good on that back street. Just follow me," he said, leading her across the street.

Mr. Jackson and three of his customers had been watching the whole mess with Lou and Mr. Morgan from the front window of his barbershop.

As Johnny and Lou approached, Mr. Jackson swung the door open and said, "The answer is yes."

"But you don't even know what the question is gonna be yet, Mr. Jackson," Johnny said, almost grinning.

"Yes, I do. You need a new spot. We would love to have you in front of Jackson's. I called your house this morning to see if you were sick or something when I saw Susie Brewster setting up in front of the bank. Bets said you and your Mom had already left. I knew that very minute there was going to be trouble. I had seen Susie go in and out of the bank several times this week to see her Grandpa. Looks like she had it planned pretty well."

"Yeah, well, I'm moving on now. It's not as bad as getting hit with a Big Mel fastball, and I have survived a few of those. She might have the best spot, but yours is a pretty good spot, too. And besides, I have a secret weapon," Johnny reasoned as calm was now returning to the situation.

"Oh really," Lou said, beginning to feel better about Johnny's situation and sensing his attitude was strong enough to handle what had just happened. "What's your secret weapon?"

"Mom, if you will go down to Griff's Rexall and get me another poster board, I will unload the van and get set up. I will show you my secret weapon in a few minutes. Stop worrying already—everything is gonna be fine," Johnny said to Lou, who was getting back to normal after that high-noon moment with Mr. Morgan that had caused her blood pressure to explode.

Lou returned in a few minutes with a fresh poster board just as Johnny finished setting up the stand. He hadn't even noticed that Susie was already open and serving customers across the street.

Johnny laid the poster board on the table and wrote out the secret weapon:

"FEATURING MISS DARLENE'S SPECIAL RECIPE"

Johnny held up the sign so Lou and Mr. Jackson could get a good look, and both smiled and nodded with approval. This was truly a great secret weapon as everybody in town had sat at Miss Darlene's kitchen counter and had her lemonade at one time or another.

Johnny was brilliant. Susie might have stolen his spot, but Johnny's Lemonade Stand had the best product in town, and he was going to let everybody know it.

As soon as the sign went up, customers started heading in his direction. By ten o'clock in the morning, he had sold thirty cups, and he was feeling good again about his lemonade business. He had just survived his first major business crisis under some intense pressure.

At ten thirty, four carloads of girls pulled up in front of the stand and started unloading.

"Where's Bets?" VJ shouted over the talkative group.

"I'm coming," Bets yelled back as she came around the corner with another huge group of girls.

"What are ya'll doing?" Johnny asked Bets as she came walking up to the stand.

"We are here to buy the best lemonade in Belleville," Bets said, smiling at Johnny.

"You're kidding me, right?"

"Did you think I was going to let Susie Brewster run my brother out of the lemonade business without a fight? Mr. Jackson told me what happened this morning. Give every one of these girls a tall glass, and give me the bill, Johnny. I think there's twenty-eight of us in all."

"Bets, that's a lot of money; you don't have to do this."

"Johnny, that's what big sisters are for. Now start pouring."

Johnny gleefully obliged and couldn't help but think about Bets in a whole new light. She really did love her baby brother after all, even if she did have some strange ways of showing it.

Bets and her group hung around for a while. The size of her group seemed to create some excitement and helped draw in some other customers.

At noon, Johnny was on about the same sales pace as he had been the previous Saturday, which was an amazing success given all the changes that had taken place in his business over the past few hours.

As the afternoon approached one thirty, Johnny noticed Susie beginning to dismantle her lemonade stand. He figured she just didn't have the stamina to go the distance.

At about two o'clock, Lou came by and told Johnny she was going over to speak with Mr. Morgan. She said she wanted to apologize for overreacting to the situation. Besides, she said, "all's well that ends well."

Even though the situation with Mr. Morgan had made her angry, Lou knew that Johnny had responded well and had shown maturity and a canny ability to make a good decision quickly. She was very proud of the way he had kept his cool and remained calm.

When she got back from the bank, she said Mr. Morgan had accepted her apology and offered one of his own. She told Johnny his offer was still good for splitting time each month with Susie in front of the bank if he wanted to do that.

She said Mr. Morgan told her that Susie had sold about ninety cups of lemonade before she had to pack it in and go to a baby shower for her Aunt Kate.

Johnny really felt good now because he had sold 145 cups in front of Mr. Jackson's barber shop. His customers had really stuck with him, even after his abrupt move.

As he and Lou were loading up the lemonade stand, Mr. Jackson came out onto the sidewalk and asked Johnny if he could speak to him privately.

"Sure," Johnny agreed, not knowing what was coming next.

"I just wanted you to know that you have what it takes to be a very good businessman, Johnny. I was very impressed with the way you handled yourself today. Most adults would have just called it quits after that unexpected disaster, but here you are, a fourteen-year-old kid, and you just worked right through it like a seasoned pro. You've got the big three, Johnny. You've definitely got the big three," Mr. Jackson told Johnny with a serious, but pleasant, look on his face.

"Do you mean the three legs of the stool?" Johnny asked, looking puzzled.

"No," Mr. Jackson replied. "The three legs of the stool—product, capital, and customers—are just the infrastructure of any business. I mean the three things that sit on top of the stool to make any business flourish. But I have to get back to my next cut now. You come by next week, and I will tell you all about the big three."

"How about next Wednesday afternoon?" Johnny asked as he got back to helping Lou load the van. "I'm sure I will have some stories of my own to tell after Tuesday's opening day game against Big Mel and the Buzzards."

"Sure thing, Johnny, I will see you next Wednesday. Good luck against the Buzzards," Mr. Jackson said as he disappeared back into his shop.

Johnny and Lou had a quiet ride home after what had been a very stressful day at Johnny's Lemonade Stand, albeit in the end, a very good day.

After they finished unloading the van, Johnny thanked his mom again for all she had done to help him keep his lemonade business alive and well.

Lou gave him a big hug and told him how proud she was of the new businessman who lived in her house. She assured him she would never lose her cool again as she had done earlier in the day with Mr. Morgan.

"Are you kidding? That was priceless," Johnny said, grinning.

"Yeah Mom, I heard you really lowered the boom on Mr. Morgan today. Wish I had seen that," Bets chuckled as she walked through the family room.

"Oh, it was nothing. We made up, and everything is fine now."

"Hey Bets, have you seen my glove?" Johnny asked as Bets plopped down on the sofa.

"Yeah, I saw it last week on your hand."

Bets was now officially done with being nice to Johnny. Her attitude was back and order had returned to the Universe. Johnny just rolled his eyes and headed to the bottomless hall corner.

He had so much to look forward to: another trip to Castle Mountain, opening day of baseball season, that visit he planned with Mr. Jackson, and another week of Johnny's Lemonade Stand.

But as much as some things had changed in Johnny's life, one thing had remained the same, he had lost his baseball glove again.

"Mom, have you seen my..."

"You find what you're looking for, Johnny!"